SUSIE FAUX

# WARDROBE

SOLUTIONS

SUSIE FAUX

# WARDROBE

## SOLUTIONS

*a total system for dressing with style and confidence*

MARSHALL PUBLISHING • LONDON

A Marshall Edition
Conceived, edited and designed by
Marshall Editions Ltd
The Orangery
161 New Bond Street
London W1Y 9PA

First published in the UK in 1999 by Marshall Publishing Ltd

ISBN 1-84028-282-7

Originated in Italy by Articolor
Printed and bound in Italy by New Interlitho Spa

Art editor  Joanna Stawarz
Editor Antonia Cunningham
Managing art editor  Helen Spencer
Managing editor  Clare Currie
Editorial director Ellen Dupont
Art director  Dave Goodman
DTP editor  Lesley Gilbert
Editorial coordinator  Becca Clunes
Production  Nikki Ingram, Sarah Hinks

*To Dad and Grandpa, for their influence on my style
and perfectionism. And to my husband Victor,
for all his love, support and press cuttings.
To all Ladybirds!*

# Contents

# Introduction

*I have written* Wardrobe Solutions *for everyone who would like to share my experience. It will serve as an insightful reference and style guide for those of you who are starting out on your career and want be as competitive as you possibly can. It will help those of you who, like I did, want to return to work after years of looking after children but have lost your confidence and feel out of touch. It will also act as a quiet reminder for those of you who are at home most of the time and know just how easy it is to get stuck in a rut. And for the older generation who may now have the time to experiment with clothes and make-up, but who are ignored by most of the shops, magazines and designers – this book should be a welcome source of information and advice.*

*For over 25 years I have helped woman gain confidence and now I have realized my dream by creating a sanctuary where women from all walks of life can be advised, dressed, accessorized, groomed and pampered, all under one roof. My aim has always been to turn shopping into a pleasurable experience instead of the usual nightmare.*

*My passion for clothes was already well developed at the grand old age of eight, when my pocket money was earned by sewing hems for my father and grandfather's workshop. They were both master tailors and good teachers.*

*By the age of 12, a Saturday job had brought me my first pair of pearly-pink winklepickers. But these were not to be my final fashion "faux-pas". When I came home wearing a rabbit coat a year later (every girl had one, of course) my grandfather took one look at me and, in broken English, exclaimed, "From this, you catch disease!" I was brought up to believe that one saved to buy good quality rather than spending money on clothes that were cheap and that would not last. As the saying goes, "you have to be rich to buy cheap". And this continues to be my belief today – a few clothes of good quality are all a woman needs to achieve a confident appearance.*

*Looking at a beautifully made garment gives me the same thrill as standing before a lovely painting – they are both works by craftsmen. By the time you've finished reading this book you will only buy clothes that suit you, fit you and, above all, you will buy clothes that make you feel good.*

*Watching a woman blossom as she realizes her full potential by putting the "fashion jigsaw puzzle" together in a way that is right for her is the reason that I love my job. It's a passion that I want to share with all of you.*

# Psychology of Appearance

*Clothes are an amazingly powerful tool. They can give us confidence and can persuade others to have confidence in us – never underestimate what your appearance says about you.*

Everyday, as women of all professions, ages and sizes enter Wardrobe, I observe what they wear and subconsciously evaluate their personalities. Over the years I have realised that the way a woman dresses is directly linked to her personal level of confidence. In this chapter I'd like to share a few of my observations with you.

## DRESSING FOR THE WRONG KIND OF ATTENTION

One day a woman came into the shop dressed in a leopard-print, fur waistcoat, an electric-blue skirt, a red sweater with a white feather boa wrapped around the neck, royal-blue tights and navy shoes. I honestly thought it was a joke. As we began to talk, she explained. "I know I'm not attractive but if I dress like this at least I know people will look at me." Her honesty touched me. This woman revealed what thousands of others would never dare to. Most of the women in the world who dress in flamboyant, even outrageous, clothing (and colours) are really dressing to attract attention. They lack the confidence to be themselves.

However, every woman in the world, no matter what age, size or shape can develop her own style while still being fashionable. There's no denying that those of you who are not an "average" shape (very tall, very thin, very fat or very small) will find it more difficult and probably more expensive to dress well – we all know that most shops around the world cater for "average" sizes and if you aren't an average size, the choice is limited. But don't be disheartened. By working in a more focused way on getting the right look for yourself, you'll look that much better, believe me.

## CONFIDENCE, CONFIDENCE, CONFIDENCE

There have been at least three times in my life when I have experienced a direction dilemma. By that, I mean times when I've

### A FRIEND IN NEED...

Finding an honest friend is vital. It doesn't have to be someone with whom you socialize on a regular basis. In fact, someone who works in a shop or beauty parlour is often better. What is important is that you trust that person to tell you the truth and having been told the truth you won't get upset by it.

> *' ... we read off the many signals that our companions' clothes transmit to us in every social encounter. In this way clothing is as much a part of human body-language as gestures, facial expressions and postures. '*
>
> DESMOND MORRIS, *MANWATCHING*

felt the need to reassess my personal style. Many things in life can trigger such a feeling, regardless of whether they are sad or happy events. Bereavement, divorce, career relocation, marriage are all rites of passage and need to be recognised as such ... Let me explain. My first direction dilemma occured when I was 16, looking for my first job with very few qualifications to my name. It was the first time I realized how important appearance was.

The second direction dilemma came soon after my first son was born. Slightly overweight and lacking in confidence I decided to head in the direction of a stylish shop. As I looked longingly at a selection of designer clothes, an assistant pulled me towards a less expensive range and said "Your rail is over there, dear". The idea of Wardrobe was born that very afternoon. My dream would be to run a clothing shop that inspired confidence, and I promised myself that no one would ever leave its premises feeling as awful as I did that day.

**There are at least three times in my life when I've felt the need to reassess my personal style.**

The third was when I heard with great joy and excitement that I was going to be a grandmother. I was surprised by how I felt – true excitement, great, great joy but also an unmistakable "ping" inside. I just didn't feel old enough to be a grandmother and I certainly wasn't old enough to assume the traditional granny image. So, in search of direction again, I went on a shopping spree and was shown how, with a little less make-up and softer hair, today's grannies can be made from quite a different mould.

Why am I telling you all this? Because at three different stages of my life I learnt that confidence is the key to looking good. Whatever

> ' *Why do fashions in clothes change? Because, really, we ourselves change in the slow metamorphoses of time. If we imagine ourselves now in the clothes we wore six years ago, we shall see that it is impossible.* '
>
> D.H. Lawrence, Writer 1885–1930

makes you feel wonderful, whatever boosts your mood, do it – whether it means wearing heels, buying a new lipstick, having a massage or wearing a different colour. Whatever works, just do it!

Which brings me to what I call "The Decade Dump". Women (and men) tend to view important birthdays with a certain amount of trepidation, which isn't surprising when we hear common phrases such as "reaching the big 4-0" or "I'm middle-aged now". I invented the Decade Dump philosophy when I realized how important each new decade was. Instead of entering your 30s, 40s, 50s and so on with feelings of doom and gloom, see it as a time to re-evaluate yourself. Literally dump the decade you've just lived through and style yourself appropriately for the next. This may involve a shorter hairstyle, wearing less make-up, or a wardrobe evaluation. Why is this so important? Because by making subtle changes you will avoid potentially depressing comparisons like "That was me then and this is me now, exactly the same only with a few more wrinkles and grey hairs." You only need to look around at some of the most stylish older women in the world to see how this philosophy really works. Take Raquel Welch, for example. If she were to wear the same heavy eyeliner and long, flowing hair now, as she did in the 50s, she would just look like an ageing version of the star she was. Instead, with every new decade she has made changes to her style (shorter hair, sharper clothes, less dramatic makeup) to look the very best she can for her age today. The message is clear. Forget trying to cling on to what you once were, style yourself for who you are now.

## Recognizing What Makes you Feel Good

Recognizing your own shape is of course the first step to looking good (see pp. 34–35). As the saying goes, knowledge breeds power

### FIND YOUR OWN "I'M FABULOUS" GARMENT

Everyone has got one garment in their wardrobe that they reach for when they need a boost. Is it a little black dress? Is it a fabulous pair of trousers? Pull yours out of the wardrobe and take a good look at it. Ask yourself what it is about that garment that gives you confidence. Is it the colour, the shape, the length of the skirt or the width of the trouser? Once you've determined what it is, you'll be able to shop for more "feel-good" garments with greater confidence.

and power can make us feel very confident. Once you've got a basic idea of the kind of clothes that are most likely to suit you, read on to find some other ways to make yourself feel good.

## LOOKING GOOD TO FEEL GOOD

When you're happy about your shape and size, your confidence is at an all-time high. Therefore, it's important to recognize that the effort that goes into getting your shape right is never wasted. Taking exercise and having a balanced, healthy diet not only gets your body into good shape, but also boosts your energy levels and self-esteem. No amount of clothing is going to make you feel good about yourself if, when you're undressed, you feel miserable.

If you want to lose weight to improve your self-esteem, the first step towards success is to buy clothes that make you feel glamorous *now*. I often hear "When I've lost the weight, I'll buy the suit." The woman who says that never loses the weight. If she buys a suit that makes her feel great for the size she is now, she feels good about herself immediately and wants to feel even better – the best kind of encouragement a woman needs to lose weight.

## THE POWER TO CHANGE OUR SELF-PERCEPTION

A woman came in to see me one day saying she wanted to look glamorous. At the end of our meeting she said rather accusingly, "You sold me beautiful clothes and I looked the best I've ever looked but you didn't change the shape of my body. I've still got sloping shoulders and my hips are still wide." Clothes can camouflage, they can provide glamour, but they can't change your physical shape. However, it's surprising to see how many women believe that when they remove glamorous clothes, somehow the glamour will remain. Of course, the body looks the same as it did before the clothes were put on. The woman in question loved the person she became when she put on her new clothes. What she didn't realize was the extent to which clothes have the power to change the way we feel about ourselves. Make the most of that, but never lose sight of who you really are. Don't treat clothes as armour. It's vital to let the real you shine through.

... clothes have the power to change the way we feel about ourselves.

# Taking a Look at Yourself

❖

*The key to looking good is accepting your body, learning how to emphasize its good points, and camouflaging those you are less happy with.*

# First Impressions

*When I meet someone for the first time, it's what I call "the moment of truth". We decide whether we appear friendly or hostile, cordial or aloof, stylish or frumpy – the positives and negatives of human behaviour.*

Of course that initial judgement may be disproved later as we get to know each other better but if the impression we get is negative, we may never actually bother to go beyond the stage of that initial meeting.

## THE MOMENT OF TRUTH

Faced with a room full of strangers I become one of life's shy people. From my experience there are only two ways of dealing with this problem: first, a warm and friendly smile; second, wearing the clothes that give me the maximum amount of confidence. So first impressions or "the moment of truth" are extremely important. And this applies to both our personal and professional lives.

In my opinion, British and American women often lag far behind the Italian and French in the sartorial stakes. To the more cosmopolitan Europeans, the British woman may look freaky or frumpy, displaying a lack of attention to clothes, hair and make-up. On the other hand, American women tend to overdress or stick to a work uniform, which, however stylish, denies individuality.

Now that more women have started up the career ladder, it is vital to realise that one of the additional factors that will set them ahead is the ability to dress well, in a way that demonstrates responsibility, credibility and confidence.

It's interesting that in the past, academics were almost expected to look scruffy – the absent-minded professor and the impoverished student. Now, in an increasingly competitive job market, employment-seeking undergraduates are realizing their abilities can only be enhanced by presenting a good appearance.

We are so strongly visually orientated that the choice we display by our appearance always makes a statement. In this book, I hope to give you guidelines on how to make this the very best sort of declaration of yourself.

*' Not caring how you look is but a brief step away from not caring what you do or how you treat people. And surely, if you treat yourself with contempt, you're going to have little thought, care or compassion for anybody else. '*

LYNDA LEE POTTER
JOURNALIST FOR *THE DAILY MAIL*

14

## BE YOUR OWN BEST ADVERTISEMENT

If you like yourself, it shows in the way you look. We all know that it's much easier to like someone if they obviously like themselves. Similarly, if someone sees themselves as a long-suffering drudge they'll start to look like one. It's a self-perpetuating vicious circle: the lower a person's self esteem, the worse they look. The worse they look, the lower the regard they receive from others. A person's depression is often revealed through their appearance. It is, therefore, crucial to care about the way you look.

Too many women feel guilty about indulging themselves. During a very stressful period of my life, my husband was forever telling me to have my guilt surgically removed. Now when I'm feeling down or stressed, I make a point of pampering myself. This is time for myself, by myself and it's the very best therapy.

Modern science can perform "miracles" on our naked selves – we can fake-tan our skins, have hair removed, lift faces and breasts, tuck our tummies – but these treatments are not all cheap, painless or safe. Clothes, however, provide a pain-free, completely safe and relatively cheap way to change your shape.

Recognize that your appearance does count and use it to boost your confidence both in yourself and in your abilities. It is undoubtedly one of your most powerful means of communication, so be smart, in both senses of the word, and be your own best advertisement to the outside world.

## IN A MATTER OF SECONDS …

It is often said that first impressions are made in three minutes. Wrong. I believe that they are made in a matter of seconds. When I walk into a room to meet a prospective employee, the very first thing I notice is the way that the person looks. If they are going to represent my company, I require them to look good and understand the necessity of giving a credible, approachable and friendly appearance. I also want them to look confident and successful. Unless they learn otherwise, people will accept the image of yourself that you give them – if you look chic and successful, they will

### LOOKING GOOD AT THE TOP

The better you look, the more you will be thrust into prominence, whether meeting the public, new clients or the media, or being asked to make presentations. If you are confident in your appearance, this gives you an opportunity to impress clients and colleagues as well as prospective employers or employees. If you are the interviewer, you are a highly paid visual representative of your company so it is important to present an attractive image to encourage the very best candidates to want to work for you. Many jobs advertised today demand "excellent communication skills", and many companies run training programmes to refine these qualities in their employees. However, when you walk into a room full of strangers, the most immediate and direct instrument of communication that you have at your disposal is your appearance.

15

**It is often said that first impressions are made in three minutes. Wrong. I believe they are made in a matter of seconds.**

believe that you are chic and successful. Never be under the illusion that the person whom you are meeting (whether it be a potential boss, husband or friend) will dismiss the visual you. If you present a poor appearance, it is much harder to convince them that you are creative or more successful than you look.

This is particularly important for those who work in public service. An aspiring politician once told me that she could not present herself as a smart professional – which she was – because this would widen the gulf between herself and the electorate in a depressed, inner-city area. But, of course, a voter who wants to put trust and hope in a politician is far more likely to do so for someone who looks successful and credible than someone who looks downtrodden. We frequently seek "role models" we can admire and aspire to and the voter is bound to think, "if she can do that for herself, surely she can do something for me!" A professional appearance does not imply lack of sympathy. If you are really ill, which doctor would you rather see – the unkempt, casually dressed one or the one sitting in a smart office looking good? An impressive appearance will never compensate for a lack of ability, but dressing smartly does induce confidence and trust. There is no doubt that it will help you in whatever you wish to achieve.

### CLOTHES *DO* THE PROFESSIONAL WOMAN MAKE

A customer once asked me, "Why do I always get asked to make the coffee when I go into a boardroom meeting?" She was a highly qualified young accountant. I suggested we look in the mirror and I asked her to describe herself candidly. We both agreed that an ill-fitting jacket with a frumpy skirt did not help her image. Exchanging them for a smartly tailored suit and stylish shoes with more fashionable hair and make-up was a revelation.

I always advise women to dress for a job that is one position higher than their own, particularly if they are starting a new career.

I always advise women to dress for a job that is one position higher than their own, particularly if they are starting a new career. A personnel director witnessed the transformation of five women who came into Wardrobe for style advice. Afterwards she admitted

16

## PEOPLE BELIEVE WHAT YOU TELL THEM

Unless there is proof to the contrary, people generally believe what you tell them about yourself. If you run yourself down, your acquaintances will believe what you say; if you seem confident they will presume that you are efficient and capable. Inevitably, your approach will determine the reaction that you get. The same is true of your clothes, a fact that institutions such as the police and the judiciary have understood for many years. Why else does a judge wear a wig and a gown but to look authoritative and imposing? Even if you are not very interested in clothes, you should remember that you can do yourself a lot of favours by bothering with your appearance.

‘ *Employers are quite willing to pay more
for people who already look the part. There
is the inference that employees who care about
themselves will care about their jobs.* ’

SUSAN BIXLER, *THE PROFESSIONAL IMAGE*

that she had at first been sceptical of my belief in the power of well-made clothes. Looking at the women now, she realized she would be embarrassed to offer them the salary she had originally planned and would now offer them significantly more. They looked as though they deserved it.

## "POWER DRESSING"

The term "power dressing" has often been discussed with derision by the press. I like to think of it more as "responsibility dressing". There is no doubt that if you want a successful career, this involves taking responsibility and the judicious use, rather than abuse, of power. It shouldn't ever involve aggression, intimidation or ruthlessness. Power and femininity are not incompatible. So ignore those who mock you for responsibility dressing – they almost certainly carry a sneaking suspicion that had they improved their appearance their chances of success would have been increased.

Similarly customers sometimes tell me that they couldn't polish up their appearance because their boss would resent it. In my experience, the more enlightened female boss is likely to ask you where you got your new look – and go there herself! If she is disparaging, then she is probably insecure about her own appearance and, more importantly, her ability to keep her job and is unlikely to promote you anyway. As my husband, a management consultant and business school professor says, "First-rate managers hire first-rate people; second-rate managers hire third-rate people." So remember, if you look like a first-rate individual, you are far more likely to be hired by a first-rate manager. When a position needs filling, your appearance could help you leap-frog over your less professional-looking peers and give your manager a subtle prod in your direction!

**TIPS**

● You must feel comfortable in your clothes. It can undermine your confidence and distract you if you're worried about how you look or feel. If you are in a meeting in a skirt that is too tight or too short you will feel uncomfortable both physically and psychologically. If you feel confident that the way you look is appropriate, your mind can concentrate purely on the business in hand.

● I frequently hear women say, "I'll buy the outfit when I get the job." My reply is always, "Buy the outfit to get the job."

# The Language of Clothes

*There are still plenty of prejudices against women in the workplace and not to capitalize on your sartorial potential is foolhardy. Do not make the mistake of thinking it an unimportant luxury. Presentation matters.*

To overcome any prejudice against you as a woman in the workforce, you need to look and feel secure and comfortable in your role as a professional rather than sending out signals that you don't belong.

### THE PROFESSIONAL WOMAN

If men have been brought up to believe that a woman's place is in the home then they can find working women an unknown quantity. I once overheard a man at a business school remarking on a group of women about to embark on a course, "Do you see those intimidating women?" he asked a colleague, a note of alarm in his voice. The group of women to which he was referring was the most unassuming and ill-groomed imaginable! He was seeing them in the knowledge that they were women in business, and had a strong preconceived prejudice against them. Although the existence of high-achieving career women is no longer a rarity, the *idea* of such women can still cause an element of discomfort among men.

I think that women are too sensitive about looking intimidating, and confuse looking sharp with appearing competent and capable. Looking smart will signify that you know how to present yourself – that you are competent in your grooming – and this, in turn, will influence others in making an assessment of your competence in other areas. As a male lawyer once said to me, "A woman who looks good and is intelligent and articulate is dynamite in any organisation."

There exist certain cultures that have a strange attitude to success. "Success" and "ambition" have been words tainted with distrust and even distaste, particularly when applied to women. It's as if these qualities have to be associated with an unacceptably aggressive manner, and that qualifications will speak for themselves.

**Looking smart will signify that you know how to present yourself, that you are competent in your grooming ...**

**NIGHTLY ORGANISATION**

Five minutes spent every night deciding what to wear the next day and sorting out what you need is five minutes well spent and will minimize any potential wardrobe crises the next morning. Make sure your clothes are clean and pressed and that your hosiery is ladder-free. Pick out the right shoes, handbag, any jewellery and even your underwear. For those who aren't at their best in the morning (myself included) these nightly five minutes are truly valuable and are a great stress reliever.

Regrettably, any attempt to look successful tends to be dismissed as vanity. Some women seem to think that if they give the appearance of being too successful, they've got further to fall if they fail. In fact, they believe that an unassuming appearance can act as a safety net as no one will expect too much from them. However, people are now beginning to realize that it's alright to be ambitious and that a confident appearance can help you get to the top of your field.

> Some women seem to think that if they give the appearance of being too successful, they've got further to fall if they fail.

The success or failure of your professional life can affect your personal life. Some men, even today, find it emasculating to be with a woman who is more successful than they are. Many women try to play down such success by looking dowdy – a ploy that doesn't really work. Looking uncoordinated or harassed and fraught (even if you are) will only reinforce the impression that you can't handle responsibility and pressure.

## EXCUSES, EXCUSES

Over the years, many of my customers both in the shop and at my seminars have given reasons why they avoid improving the way they look. Here are some of their more frequent justifications.

### "I COULDN'T SPEND THE MONEY"

You often feel guilty about spending money on yourself. Conditioning often leads you to expect others to be dependent on you – husbands, children or perhaps even parents. You spend money on what are considered to be the necessities – food, clothes for the children, cars, holidays abroad and school fees. You feel guilty about spending money on yourself; somehow it's far easier to justify buying a household gadget. If you buy something for yourself it's best if it's a bargain.

Do you delight in telling others the cost of a garment bought in a sale – but keep very quiet if you've spent rather a lot of money on it? In contrast, Italian and French women feel guilty if they do not buy good clothes or have a regular manicure. By investing in your appearance, you are also investing in your professional future and, with any luck, you are enjoying yourself in the process too. Your financial success and rewards are going to come from your career.

19

**DRESS FOR A BETTER JOB**

If you're ambitious and career-minded, always dress for a job one position higher than the one you are interviewing for. If you're a secretary, dress as a PA. If you're an account manager, dress as an account director, and so on. If the position that you are after becomes vacant, you'll stand a better chance of being offered the job because you already look the part.

Therefore, buying a professional wardrobe should be part and parcel of your working life. Never see it is as an extravagance – rather as a necessity.

"I DON'T HAVE THE TIME"

Caring about your looks can easily be relegated to low priority, especially if you have a job to do, a home to run and a husband and children to feed and clothe. You feel guilty about spending time – personal shopping time – when there seem to be so many other important things to do.

Trying to add to a badly managed wardrobe can be very time-consuming. It is often difficult to find an appropriate item to fit in with an overly large and haphazard collection of clothes; clothes often bought on impulse or in the sales. This book aims to show you how to save time by training your eye, using the criteria of cut, cloth and colour when you buy. In business you operate most effectively by taking time to consider action rather than by charging in and behaving rashly. Your wardrobe should be run along similar lines because a successful wardrobe is a result of careful planning and projection.

Sometimes, if you feel that a particularly large number of demands are being made on you by family and friends, visibly demonstrating a lack of concern for your appearance can act as a defence. If you dress in a jumble of shapes and colours you are not likely to exude confidence and are, therefore, less likely to be asked by your colleagues at work to shoulder greater responsibility, though you are probably quite capable of doing so.

The sad fact is that the longer you continue to ignore your appearance, the more inadequate you will feel and become. Start to think and act constructively about the way you look and you will find other people (and yourself) responding more positively. Perhaps you have been avoiding making your appearance matter because you have a sneaking suspicion that your abilities cannot match up to it? Are you afraid that if you were given more

> In business you operate most effectively by taking time to consider action rather than by charging in and behaving rashly. Your wardrobe should be run along similar lines.

'*I think the fact that women are noticed in business more than men is because there are less of us around ... It's an opportunity for us to stand out and make our mark ... Women should feel positive about this.* '

JAN PESTER, MARKETING DIRECTOR

responsibility you couldn't live up to expectations? If so, you need to investigate ways of building your confidence and self-esteem.

## "WHAT WILL PEOPLE SAY?"

If you start to take your appearance seriously and change your look, your work colleagues are likely to comment on it. They may think that you're trying to get one step ahead of them and they may well be right! Be prepared for comments such as, "So who are you trying to impress?" When you hear such negative remarks – remarks often born out of jealousy – the simplest response is, "I haven't got time to mess about in the morning so I've decided to adopt an easier way of dressing. Getting myself together makes my life easier." A good way of judging your female boss is to study her reaction when you change your appearance. A confident boss will be delighted if her subordinates look good because it reflects on her. She'll be the kind of boss who will enjoy helping you progress. Remember my husband's theory: first-rate managers hire first-rate staff, second-rate managers hire third-rate staff – usually because they feel insecure about their own careers.

## "BUT I DON'T WANT TO SEEM VAIN"

Most of us would hate to be thought of as vain and self-obsessed. Indeed, people who are constantly thinking and talking about their appearance are pretty boring. They tend to have immature personalities because their identity is completely defined by their looks. Self-obsession and vanity arise from insecurity and are quite different from self-esteem, which arises from confidence and a balanced view of your achievements and shortcomings. Self-esteem is reflected in your appearance and also in the way you present yourself to family, friends and colleagues.

### BUT I *DO* WANT TO BE TAKEN SERIOUSLY

You might feel that what you do is far more important than how you look. However, there is no doubt that today's successful and well-dressed women are powerful. Whether we like it or not, the way a professional woman dresses counts for more than for her male colleagues. Whereas the least clothes-conscious of men can achieve high office, the same cannot be said for women. An internationally renowned business school recently carried out a survey to find out to what extent a professional woman's wardrobe mattered. Out of ten female MBA students, five listed their appearance as a top priority. The remaining five claimed they didn't pay much attention to their appearance. Five years later, the study concluded that those who had made the effort were far more successful than those who hadn't considered it a priority.

21

## WOMEN AT HOME

It is always a mistake to assume that women with careers are the ones who should look good and that the way non-career women dress doesn't matter. As far as I'm concerned, the difference between a career woman and a housewife is that a career woman is paid for her job. This is the factor that causes many housewives to lack self-esteem. I often hear women say, "How can I justify spending that amount of money on clothes when I'm not earning it?" It is my belief that every woman can.

> As far as I'm concerned, the difference between a career women and a housewife is that a career woman is paid for her job.

Being at home doesn't mean you can't be fashionable. Never feel guilty about buying stylish clothes or paying regular visits to a beautician. You may not be working outside the home but you *are* working. If you spend your time at home with the children, you still have the need to look good, and if you don't spend time looking after yourself, your confidence is sure to plummet. Instead of feeling depressed, visit the hairdresser regularly or, if money is tight, go to a hairdresser on a model night (choose your salon carefully) – the best will always insist on a senior stylist monitoring your cut. In other words, do all that is necessary to make yourself feel good.

Remember you have responsibilities and are part of a partnership. Just because you are not carrying out the role of wage-earner, doesn't mean that you should be denied the right to look good. As a housewife, you don't receive payment in terms of a salary but it is still important that you view your wardrobe and personal upkeep in the same way as a career woman does – as a necessity.

> *'Put the plainest woman into a beautiful dress and unconsciously she will try to live up to it.'*
> LADY DUFF GORDON, *WOMEN'S JOURNAL*, 1944

### THE LEGGING SYNDROME

It is, however, very easy if you are at home, particularly with small children, to relegate your appearance to the bottom of your list of priorities. You may not socialize much and apart from anything else, you may feel too busy and too tired to even want to think about what you are wearing. It's very easy to end up, day after day, in a pair of leggings, a T-shirt and a sweater. This will do nothing to boost your morale, especially if you are feeling at a low ebb. When I was a young mother at home, I soon realised that what I looked like contributed to my mood and feelings of being able to cope. Just because you need no-fuss clothes, does not mean that you have to lose your sense of style. If you choose classic styles that mix and match well and are easy to care for, you can be comfortable, throw things in the washing machine at the drop of a hat, stretch and bend as much as you like, and still look good. And remember that you deserve a few minutes each day for yourself – even if it is only to take the time to wash and dry your hair or put on your makeup.

## GETTING ORGANIZED

It is important to allow yourself some time to care about your clothes and to organize regular appointments with your hairdresser and beautician. I find it helpful to make appointments well in advance – sometimes even up to six months. Even if I have to change them, those meetings are in my diary and they are *my personal time.*

As far as clothes are concerned, I advise my customers to put aside half a day twice a year to update and add to their wardrobe rather than buying a jacket or a skirt at odd times during the year and running the risk of nothing really coordinating. You may feel daunted at the prospect of doing this on your own. If so, let someone else help. Find a reliable shopping advisor, preferably at your local boutique or department store, if you prefer, whom you can trust. This is often a service provided free of charge. Knowing that you are organized will take away the strain and make you feel more secure.

Many women fall into the trap of feeling guilty about asking for help. They think they should know how to dress. However, most women are not born with an innate sense of style and, just as I wouldn't consider myself qualified to solve a legal issue, I wouldn't expect a customer to know exactly how to organize her wardrobe. The best-dressed women are the ones who will ask for advice, as they are aware of what they don't know. The women who say, "I know what suits me", and are not open to suggestions become stuck in a rut. They cannot possibly know as much about what is on offer or be as knowledgeable as someone whose career it is. Always be open to new ideas – you may be surprised.

**The best-dressed women are the ones who are prepared to ask for advice, as they are aware of what they don't know.**

### KEEPING UP WITH FASHION

The easiest way to ensure that your wardrobe is up to date is by reading fashion magazines. There is no need to take each season's new look literally and become a fashion victim. It's simply a question of staying tuned. I always advocate dressing on the classic side of fashionable. The capsule wardrobe and other principles of dressing discussed throughout this book apply to everyone, regardless of whether you're a city high-flyer, corporate wife or a mum at home with young children.

23

# Beauty & Nutrition

*However stylish your wardrobe, you will not maximize your potential if you ignore the fact that hair and make-up are an intrinsic part of the fashion jigsaw.*

Even if you perfect a certain make-up look and find an attractive hairstyle, they won't suit you forever. As you change, your hair and make-up styles need to change with you if you want to make the most of yourself and build your confidence in all situations.

### MAKE-UP – MY PHILOSOPHY

A customer once said to me that she wouldn't wear make-up as she didn't have the confidence. I couldn't believe it! I wouldn't go out without make-up for the same reason. I need to feel that I am making the best of myself in order to feel confident. While I would not suggest that anyone should do anything that made them self-conscious, I think this customer misguidedly thought that wearing make-up was a sign of vanity and gave out the message, "Look at me!" My view of make-up, as with clothing, is that "Less is more", and that whatever make-up you put on should subtly enhance your features rather than draw unwanted attention to any particular part of your face. Looking your best is not a question of vanity but of self-esteem.

**What is the point of make-up if the skin no longer looks like flesh but a mask?**

The cosmetics world is so vast, many women get lost, either because they are confused by the sheer quantity of cosmetics on the market or because they get stuck in a rut and eventually give up altogether. It is important to be introduced to make-up by a recommended professional so that you are confident in the knowledge that what you are doing is right.

First and foremost, make-up should make you feel fabulous. It should also fit in with your lifestyle. Age and so-called "ordinary" looks are no excuse for not wearing the right make-up. Cosmetics are not only to enhance a woman's features, they are to be kind and helpful in any way that may be related to making her look her best and feel happy and confident.

24

**Make-up is not only for enhancing your looks but must be seen as protection for your face as well.**

Make-up should not be used as blobs of colour but as a corrective and enhancing medium. What is the point of make-up if the skin no longer looks like flesh but a mask? The eyes should not appear as a rainbow of colours but be shaped and defined; the features should be contoured and the cheeks given a natural blush. The lips should be soft, pretty to the eye, subtly enhanced and coloured to complement the occasion, your age, complexion, lip type and shape. Choose your make-up tones carefully – ask advice at a beauty counter. The consultants are trained to match products with skin tone and eye colour. Also, buy the best make-up you can – especially foundation – it makes a real difference in terms of how it lasts, looks and feels on the skin.

YOUR MAKE-UP REGIME

Because we are all subject to pollution and the ravages of the weather, make-up is not only for enhancing your looks, but must be seen as protection for your face as well. I suggest the following steps to help maintain the health and vitality of your skin.

• Good, thorough cleansing and toning of the skin, prior to moisturizing or make-up.

• An appropriate moisturizer for your skin type and age.

• A good eye and neck cream.

• Thorough removal of all traces of make-up before going to bed.

• Remember that the skin "repairs" itself at night – invest in a good night cream if you can.

Although it sounds like a lot of work, once you have established a routine, it should take no more than five minutes each night. The payback over the years will be immense. I also advise women over

| EXPIRATION DATES | |
|---|---|
| Foundation | 1-1.5 years |
| Lipstick | 1-2 years |
| Mascara | 3-4 months |
| Powder | 2 years |
| Shadows | 2 years |
| Cream cleanser | 1 year |
| Moisturiser | 1 year |

the age of 35 to have a regular facial. This moisturises the skin and expels impurities in a gentle and long-lasting way.

Applying make-up can be daunting to the uninitiated. It need not be time-consuming and once you've learnt the basics, and with a little practice, the right make-up will boost your confidence in much the same way as well-fitting clothes do. No matter who you are, regardless of your lifestyle, it's worth it for that alone. The way you achieve these ends will vary from person to person and also on the amount of time you are willing to devote to putting your make-up on in the mornings. If you don't have much time, I suggest the following steps for a fast five-minute face, which, although by no means a professional make-up, will be enough to carry you through the day:

*' There is no such thing as a plain woman. But every woman needs a good hairdresser. '*

SUSIE FAUX, STYLE CONSULTANT

- Cleanse, tone and moisturise.
- Apply light foundation, tinted moisturiser and concealer, if needed.
- Gently powder over eye area and any shiny bits.
- Blend a neutral eye shadow over the whole eye lid. If you have a shallow eyelid, blend the shadow up to the eyebrow.
- Apply mascara carefully to both your top and bottom lashes.
- Apply lipstick and then use lipliner or pencil, which will prevent your lipstick from seeping.

## HAIR CARE

Every woman has a unique beauty and it is the role of every good hairdresser to enhance it. For this to happen, a hairdresser must be just as capable of listening and understanding a woman's needs as he or she is of cutting her hair.

A hair appointment should always begin with a consultation whether you've known your hairdresser for years, or you've only just met. However, the first time you meet him or her, the consultation should be longer than usual, as your hairdresser will need to consider your face shape, skin tone, general body shape, the qualities of your hair and your lifestyle. A good hairdresser never judges from the neck up alone. Remember, use your consultation to tell your

### HAIR CONSIDERATIONS

As clothing fashions change, so too do hair fashions. You should be careful about new hair – it'll take a while to grow out if you don't like it – but don't stay stuck in the past. Above all, remember that your age and face shape are of prime importance. A good hairdresser, especially if he or she knows you, will be able to alter your style while still making sure that it suits you. Colour can also be used, either to cover up grey or to enhance aspects of your face.

26

hairdresser a bit about your lifestyle. It may be that you are a high-flying executive but have come to a salon in jeans because it is your day off. Take the time to describe as much about yourself as possible. Voice any worries you may have and discuss any changes you'd like your hairdresser to make. Never be concerned that you are being over-demanding. If you want a haircut that will suit the smart nine-to-five executive and the casually dressed mother at the weekends, a good hairdresser will deliver. He or she must also have the technical confidence and creative capability to propose different styles to enhance your features and suit your lifestyle. Never trust a hairdresser who looks to you for ideas.

How many women say, "It looked great when I came out of the hairdressers but I can't re-create the style myself?" Demonstrating techniques (how to curl hair, straighten it, applying mousse and gels) and suggesting methods of hair care and treatments are all part of a good hairdresser's job. It is vital that he or she gives you the confidence to feel as good during the weeks that you don't see them, as when you step out of their salon.

Above and below: These before and after pictures show how effective new make-up and a new haircut can be. The model's long, blonde hair had become dull and lanky and she had become accustomed to tying it back as a solution. A new haircut to her shoulders is far more manageable and shapes her face; subtle blonde highlights emphasize her eyes and skin tone; natural make-up makes her eyes and skin glow and gives colour and vitality.

27

## COLOUR

Gone are the days of peroxide blondes and harsh brunettes. Hair colour today is a safe and often indispensable tool, not only in the creation of the perfect hair style but also in helping women make the most of themselves. For instance, darkened hair will often emphasize pale eyes and vice versa.

## ... always begin with a consultation whether you've known your hairdresser for years, or you've only just met.

When I suggest hair colour to women, they often say, "but this is my natural colour." A good colourist will never insist upon change but it is important to understand that just as your skin tone changes with time, so does your hair. It may lose its natural warmth or lightness (depending on your natural colour). Hair colour can bring lightness to a tired complexion and it can take the dull appearance out of grey hair and make it sparkle instead. You can also use colour to draw attention towards or away from parts of your face. For example, highlights in the hair around your eyes will draw attention to them and away, for example, from your nose. Stronger highlights away from your face can slim down a wide face because the eye is drawn first to the colour and does not linger on the jawline. In other words, colour is the "make-up" of the hair care world. It should be used to enhance a hairstyle which then truly becomes a woman's "crowning" glory.

## A WORD OF WARNING

There are many different methods involved in colouring hair and these should be tailored to suit each individual client. Never trust a colourist who uses the same techniques day in, day out on all her customers. Just because your best friend looks great with a set of blond highlights, it doesn't mean you will. Similarly, avoid the colourist who is more interested in selling you a fashion statement, rather than giving consideration to what you really want and what is best for you.

... the food you eat, just as the clothes you buy, must be suited to your individual needs.

## NUTRITION

There is no doubt that healthy eating is essential for boosting one's energy and stamina. I am convinced that good nutrition has helped me sail through a number of the potentially stressful periods of life, and I am, therefore, constantly watching out for new and interesting ways to keep the excellent health that matters so much to me.

I don't believe in so called "diets" and I would never dream of advising any of my customers to follow one. What I do believe in is a healthy eating plan for life. Every woman's healthy eating plan will

*' Once I started drinking more water and less caffeine, I really noticed how my energy levels rose and I stopped feeling so lethargic. ,*

JOANNA DALBY, INTERNATIONAL BOOK DESIGNER

differ since we do not all benefit from or enjoy the same foods. We each have different needs and different lifestyles. Therefore, the food you eat, just as the clothes you buy, must be suited to your individual needs.

But there are a few general "common sense" guidelines to healthy eating that I follow and from which most women (and men) benefit.

I avoid coffee and tea and keep alcohol to a minimum. These drinks all have a dehydrating effect on our bodies and I know that I feel better without them. I have learnt to respect my liver as it has the important job of cleaning and filtering the blood to keep toxins under control. This means drinking plenty of clear, still water and herbal teas.

To provide me with energy that lasts all day I always eat a good breakfast including fibre such as oats or rye toast. The combination of some oats with a few nuts, seeds and apple juice is delicious and keeps me going for hours. I often eat live yoghurt since it contains friendly bacteria which keep my digestive system working properly. I aim to have carbohydrates which are high in fibre and low in simple sugar such as lentils, brown rice, beans and pulses. These give me an even level of blood sugar and hence my concentration and energy is more balanced. Sweets and chocolates, however, give a short-term boost that soon fizzles out leaving me with less energy then I had before, so I try to avoid these as much as possible and replace them with an apple mid-afternoon. I try to eat organic fruit and vegetables most days, the choice these days is so much better.

And finally, don't forget that exercise is also required for a healthy lifestyle – a little, often, is the key. It does not have to be energetic, gentle exercise will suffice. If you aren't sure what to do, consult a sports consultant at a gym or a physiotherapist, who will be able to advise you as to what is suitable.

29

## HEALTH PROBLEMS

Nutrition can also improve your immune system, digestive efficiency, hormonal balance, PMS, heart and artery health and mental concentration. The long-term prevention of many degenerative diseases such as osteoporosis, cancer, arthritis, heart disease and diabetes have all been associated with improved nutrition. Rapid improvements in stubborn problems are often made once the right approach has been found. A good nutritionist will search out the key to your health problems by using methodical analysis. Allergies or intolerances to food can also be investigated through this approach.

# Makeover *Julia*

Julia works for the Civil Service and has just been promoted. She will be running a team of several people and would like a more business-like, smart appearance.

## BEFORE

When I met Julia, she was feeling a bit dowdy and uninspired with the dark colours that she wore to the office and also rather overwhelmed by her new promotion. This seemed to be reflected in her rather diffident, round-shouldered posture. She was also hiding a lot of her face behind her hair and palid make-up gave little definition to her features. The shape of her hair added bulk and width where she least needed it around her jawline and her cheeks.

## WHAT WE DECIDED TO DO

We needed to give Julia a more stylish, business-like look that would command respect in and out of the office but would still be casual enough for her to feel comfortable and "be herself". Her hair needed to be easy to look after, but required a cut which was structured and styled away from her jawline and her forehead so that her face, especially her eyes, could be seen.

## CLOTHES

It has been my experience that when a woman puts on a garment with which she is happy, she really does stand taller. For Julia's new position of authority, we suggested she wear a trouser suit, which is more youthful and less intimidating than a formal business suit. We chose a dark suit so that Julia could use the (turn to p. 32)

30

**... her hair added bulk and width where she least needed it ...**

**VITAL STATISTICS**

Julia Osgood
**Age:** 42
**Height:** 5ft 4 in
**Dress size:** 14
**Occupation:** Civil Servant
**Aim:** To have a modern yet classic style that is easy to maintain and which makes her both approachable and credible in her professional life.

' *I was really surprised how relaxed and comfortable I felt while looking so stylish and smart* '
JULIA

**SCARF** A scarf gently tucked into a classic jacket is a stylish alternative to a blouse with a collar, or a necklace. It gives the effect of a plunging neckline, which elongates Julia's neck without being inappropriate in a working environment.

**SHIRT** A shirt with an open collar worn outside of the jacket collar has a similarly elongating effect as the scarf, but gives the suit a slightly less formal look.

31

**SUIT** A slightly longer, slim-fitting jacket with a structured shoulder line gives a defined silhouette, and balances out a somewhat heavier bottom half. The tapered trousers maintain the slimming effect on a shorter woman.

**SHOES** As a more casual alternative to the boots, a lace-up shoe is ideal. It also prevents any unsightly gaps between the shoe and the hem of the trousers.

**BOOTS** Ankle boots are the perfect complement to tapered trousers. They elongate the leg, and look better than a bare or socked ankle. The slightly chunky, higher heel gives Julia a little extra height and keeps the proportions right with the narrow trouser and tailored jacket.

jacket separately over another item of clothing such as casual trousers at the weekend. The jacket was structured and gently built up on the shoulders to even out her slightly heavy "bottom half" (see p. 35). The single-breasted style has the advantage of minimizing a larger bust, it also looks softer and is easier than a double-breasted jacket to mix and match with other items.

The trousers are a classic narrow shape that highlight Julia's good legs. A pair of heeled boots also flatter the leg, and give more height. The illusion of added height is created by the unbroken line between the boot and the hem of the trousers. Moderately high heels do help inspire self confidence in a short woman.

We softened Julia's whole look using a gently draped, blue scarf that emphasized the colour of her eyes and added a brighter touch to the suit. Styled to emphasize the "V" of her neckline, it also elongated her neck, which her round-necked top had not done.

**32**

## MAKE-UP

Julia was not used to wearing much make-up, so we gave her a natural look using a pale foundation a tone above her natural skin shade. Pale, pink and apricot eyeshadow helped to lift her eyes, and we blended it as far as the

> We softened Julia's whole look using a gently draped, blue scarf that emphasized the colour of her eyes …

> ‘ *We emphasized Julia's blue eyes by combing the hair off her face and blending light colours between her lashes and her eyebrows.* ’
> MAGGIE HUNT, MAKE-UP ARTIST

eyebrows. We then used brown mascara and eye liner to define her eyes. Brown is less harsh than black, and more suitable for paler skins.

## HAIR

Before we cut her hair, Julia had extremely thick hair styled into a slightly triangular bob that was short at the back and heavy on the top and sides. This hid her face and created downward lines that contributed to her slightly dowdy appearance.

We layered her hair to take some weight off the top and some volume from the sides, and pushed it back, which drew attention away from her jawline, giving her face more balanced length and breadth. We also decided to lift the colour of Julia's natural dull-blonde hair by adding a gloss to the hair with a vegetable dye, then combed highlights through a few strands at the front. This looks natural and flatters the complexion, and gives interest to hair texture. The blonde highlights at the front also drew attention to Julia's blue eyes – one of her best features.

### LIP SHAPING

Julia has very small lips, which she wanted to look fuller. Many women make the mistake of thinking that you can extend lips by using a lip pencil beyond the natural line of your mouth. This looks artificial and should be avoided. The best thing to do was to make Julia's lips look pretty, but then to concentrate on her eyes. It is a make-up maxim that you emphasize either the lips or the eyes, but not both. Basically, you choose to emphasize your best asset. If your lips are small and thin, then concentrate on your eyes and vice versa.

As Julia doesn't often wear make-up we chose a chestnut lip colour that we mixed with a lighter, pink shade. This created a colour that toned nicely with her hair and skin. We used a lip pencil in the same shade to outline her lips to the edges of her mouth. We then added a little gloss to make them seem more full. The result was pretty without being garish, and did not draw attention to her lips. Once you find a lip colour that you like, you may want to stick with it for the season, but if you want to experiment, coat your lips with vaseline first and then the lipstick can be easily wiped off.

# Your Body Shape

*Clothes have the magical power to accentuate the positive and eliminate the negative aspects of your body. Therefore, recognizing your body shape is the first vital step to shopping for a successful wardrobe.*

Remember, not even the world's top models are completely happy with what Mother Nature gave them. So have the courage to look at yourself completely naked. This is a real moment of truth – a very personal one that is going to show you how to feel really good about yourself for the rest of your life.

### A New Body For a New Wardrobe

If you are determined to diet or attempt to change your shape permanently then give yourself a fixed period of time in which to achieve this and implement a well-planned regime with definite goals. Never buy clothes that are too small for you with the promise that you will lose weight to fit into them. This kind of "goal-buying" never works and can be truly demoralizing. Accept your body as it is and learn to like yourself. This book is not about dressing model figures. It is about giving you confidence to make the most of who you are.

### Defining your Shape

Now you are ready to take a positive, objective and honest look at yourself. First, learn to look at yourself as a whole.

While it is vital to recognize the shape of your individual body parts, it is important that you use the body's overall shape as a constant reference. After all, you do not dress different parts of the body in different styles, you dress the whole body to create one, unified style.

Each of these factors will be discussed in this chapter, and will help you to determine the kind of clothes that you will wear.

### How to Look

Standing in front of your mirror with your hands on your waist, ask yourself the following questions:

34

### ASSESSING YOUR FIGURE

● Use a triple-way mirror so you can see what your body looks like from every angle. Make sure the mirror is straight. If any part of it is tilted your reflection will be distorted.

● Stand with your hands on your waist.

● Now look. Your eyes will automatically rest on the area of your body that you like the least or – the one that you most wish to camouflage. I call this taking an "emotional" look at yourself.

● Look again, this time taking an objective or "mental" look at yourself. Ask, "Is my bottom really huge?" In other words, forget your emotions and trust the mirror. Make it your best friend – it's the one that is going to be the most truthful.

- Do I have a small, medium or large head?
- Is my neck slim or thick?
- Do I have sloping, average or wide shoulders?
- Am I a pear shape (is your bottom half proportionally bigger than your top half)?
- Am I the shape of an inverted triangle (is your bottom half proportionally slimmer than your top half)?
- Do I have a boyish figure (straight up and down)?
- Do I have a long or short waist?
- Do I have long arms?
- Do I have a thick or narrow waist?
- Do I have shapely or bulky thighs?
- Do I have slim or thick ankles?
- Do I have slim or chunky calves?

35

## PROPORTION AND COLOUR

Very few women's bodies are perfectly in proportion. At least 50 percent of my customers have a top half that is one size and a bottom half that is another, which makes shopping for clothes, particularly suits, difficult.

Most women will either buy a suit that is a little too tight or a little too big. However, the most common mistake is to buy a jacket that fits your top half, and a pair of trousers or a skirt that fits your bottom half. Although it seems sensible to buy your clothes separately to fit certain parts of the body, this is, in fact, the worst possible thing you could do.

*... the most common mistake women make is to buy a jacket which fits their top half and trousers or a skirt which fits their bottom half.*

### WHY?

If you are a size smaller on your top half than you are on your bottom half and you buy a jacket and a skirt in the relevant sizes, the jacket may fit across the bust but it will be tight across your hips and you may have difficulty doing up the last button. You need to remember that a jacket is not cut just to fit your bust size; it is also cut to fit over your hips and, depending on its length, possibly over part or all of your bottom as well.

THE SOLUTION

Know your body's proportions. If one half of you is bigger than the other, always buy for the biggest part of the body and have either the slightly looser skirt or jacket taken in to fit. If you really want to feel confident in clothes that fit like a dream you'll need the help of a tailor or dressmaker.

IT'S NOT THE SIZE THAT COUNTS

When you're in a shop, tell the assistant the size that you think you are but don't be put off if you are handed a larger or smaller one. Every manufacturer varies in their sizing, which is why a size 12 body could be a size 10 in one shop and a size 14 in another. Ignore what the label says. What matters is that you wear clothes that fit.

WHICH COLOUR SUITS?

Contrary to popular opinion, I have never believed that people cannot wear certain colours. I would never tell a woman that she was a "winter, red person" or declare to another that she "must only wear blue". Instead I judge the suitability of a colour by the tone of a woman's skin. Once you have defined your skin tone, I believe you can wear any colour you choose, provided that you apply the right tone of make-up.

**IDENTIFYING YOUR SKIN TONE**

All skin has a yellow or pink tone, regardless of ethnic origin. European skin can be either tone, although Meditteraneans for example, are usually yellow-toned. People of African and Asian origin have skins that are based on yellow tones. But be aware that the intensity of the tone will vary from person to person.

To define your colouring first put a range of golden and earthy colours close to your face, then a range of pinks and blues and see which looks better. If you really can't tell, a beautician at a cosmetic counter should be able to help you. In the past, it has been difficult to find makeup specifically for darker skins. There are now a number of makes that specialize. Bobbi

> '*If a woman walks in and people say what a wonderful dress, she's badly dressed. If they say, there's a beautiful woman, you know she's well-dressed.*'
> ELSA SCHIAPARELLI,
> DRESS DESIGNER, 1940s

To define your colouring first put a range of golden and earthy colours close to the face, then a range of pinks and blues and see which look better.

Brown has products for yellow-based skins, with all the foundations, for example, retaining exactly the same tone, regardless of the depth of colour. Iman also caters for darker skin and Fashion Fair is designed specifically for African skins. All have a very wide range of products.

Once you have identified your skin colouring you'll learn that yellow-based colours suit golden skins and that blue-based colours look better on skins with a pink tone. However, it isn't always easy to tell because all colours are made up of many different colours. A grey, for example, could either have a yellow or blue base. Therefore, instead of saying "I can't wear grey", ask yourself which grey you're talking about. Does the grey have more blue or yellow pigment in it?

> Certain fabrics, such as velvet, have a luminosity to them and, therefore, bring light to the skin.

CHOOSING FABRIC

Experiment with different fabrics and textures. You may well find that you can wear a colour that you thought you couldn't. Certain fabrics, such as velvet, have a luminosity to them and, therefore, bring light to the skin. Others like cotton and wool can be flat and unreflective.

## SKIN TONES AND COLOUR

As a general rule, yellow or golden complexions look good in ivory, browns, earthy tones, khaki and yellow-based reds. Pink complexions suit white, navy, black, grey, pinks, lilacs, burgundy and other blue-based reds.

However, you can wear any colour of clothing if you change the tone of your skin with the judicious use of make-up. For example, my skin has a yellow base. If I want to wear fuschia pink, I use a foundation with a pink tone to it and I change my eye shadow from shades of brown to shades of grey.

Age also has a lot to do with colour. We often hear women say "I used to wear so and so, but now I don't look very good in those colours." The reason is that our skins change over the years and stronger colours are really more suited to younger complexions. If you want, you can always use bright accessories – a shawl, or a scarf – to introduce colour.

### HAIR AND CLOTHING

The colour of your hair will determine, to some extent, the colour of the clothes that you should be wearing, although I believe that skin tone is a more important factor. However, extremes of hair colour do present more of a problem. For example, redheads should avoid bright pinks but some purples can look very good. Those with yellow-blonde hair tend to look better in more golden colours but lighter blondes look good in pinks and blues. From my experience, it is less important for a brunette to consider her hair colour than her skin tone.

37

# Head, Neck & Shoulders

*Your head, neck and shoulders are the introduction to the rest of your body. Your state of mind can be interpreted through their posture. They say relaxed, stressed, proud or tired.*

They are also in the "quick-fix" part of you. Easy to transform with a new haircut, change of necklace and the use (or not) of shoulder pads.

## HEAD

If your head looks small compared to your body then a closely cut hairstyle will emphasize the contrast and your frame will look even larger. A haircut with more volume will look better. Conversely, a petite frame will be accentuated by masses of hair making the head seem bigger by comparison. Highlighting or colouring your hair can also flatter your facial features.

## HOW TO FLATTER YOUR NECK

To identify the shape of your neck, try on a number of sweaters, one with a roll neck, another with a collar and one with a longer scoop neckline, to see which one looks best.

### SHORT, THICK NECKS

If you have a short or thick neck, there are a number of things that you should, and should not, do. Long hair, for example, will emphasize a short neck, the lines of the hair shape naturally pulling the eye downwards, so a short cut is advisable. Roll collars or wide, slit necklines are also to be avoided as they create a strong line across the body at the base of the neck and draw attention to it. Cluttering the neck with short, chunky necklaces and scarves has the same effect.

To achieve an illusion of length, keep the neck as bare as possible and go for scooped and V-shaped necklines. Earrings also draw attention away from the neck. They don't have to be huge – a pretty pair of studs will do – but do make sure that they can be seen and are not hidden by your hair.

**To achieve an illusion of length, keep the neck as bare as possible and go for scooped and V-shaped necklines.**

LONG NECKS

If you have a long neck, don't wear tight roll-necks. They will emphasize the narrowness of the neck and create a disproportionate ostrich-like effect. Generous necklines with folded collars, on the other hand, create horizontal lines that cut across the neck, shortening it. Stand-up collars and reveres will also work in the same way as they add bulk to the neck area.

AGEING NECKS

If you feel that your neck is beginning to sag a bit, avoid clinging roll-neck sweaters and go for slightly scooped or shirt necklines. If you wish to wear a necklace, choose one that falls lower, drawing the eye away from the area you'd like to remain unnoticed. Don't wear chokers. If you take the time to do gentle neck exercises, you will see results and a good neck cream is a worthwhile investment.

## SHOULDERS

The shoulder line is one of the first features of the body that we notice. To wear a jacket well, you need shoulders. Even if it is not the fashion to have shoulder pads, you may wish to put a bit of padding in your jacket to add definition if your shoulders are narrow or sloping. Do be careful if you have a thin neck, though, as it will look even thinner if it is supported by excessively padded, square shoulders.

Shoulder pads are, however, a godsend for women with narrow shoulders. First, they streamline thick waists, hips and thighs by making your shape more of an inverted triangle with your hips appearing narrower than your shoulders. Second, they accentuate the shoulders, drawing the observer's eyes upwards to the head and face.

Extra padding in the shoulders will build up the shoulder line in garments such as jackets and coats but make sure you do not over-emphasize the area with heavy detail, such as epaulettes, for instance. Also, avoid raglan sleeves. These are great for women with wide shoulders with their own padding but on women whose shoulders are narrow, set-in sleeves are more flattering. Remember, exaggerated shoulders date a garment very quickly.

**TIPS**

● Disguise a disproportionately small head by maximizing the area of exposed skin between the neck and chest area. Wearing tops high up on the neck will only bring attention to the head. Try scooped and V-shaped necklines instead.

● Wide shoulders are often an asset when it comes to fashion. However, beware of halterneck-style dresses if you are bony.

● Remember, shoulder pads come in varying thicknesses and sizes. Like all accessories, they need to be in proportion to the garments in which they are worn.

● Shoulder pads can help if you have thick upper arms. If yours bulge beyond your shoulders, make sure the shoulder pad is level with the fattest part of your arm – a fashion trick that truly works.

● If your shoulders are particularly wide, padding should be minimal – if any at all.

39

# Hips & Thighs

*The one area of a woman's body most likely to give concern is the area below the waist and above the knee. It is the most difficult area to camouflage, whether you are bottom-heavy or straight up and down.*

What I always think of when I hear the words "hips" and "thighs" (and believe me I hear them a lot!) is the common problem of a woman whose wide hips make her a different size proportionally from top to bottom. Learning how to camouflage your hips and bottom is crucial – not only so that you can give the illusion of having a perfectly proportioned body but also for your own personal level of confidence.

### WIDE HIPS AND LARGE BOTTOMS

If you think that you are a bit bulky around your hips and thighs, you need to draw attention away from the bottom half of your body and emphasize the top half. You can do this by wearing shoulder pads (see p. 39), light colours, and dense, patterned or textured fabrics on your top half. Anything that pulls the eye downwards – such as belts with ornate buckles, pockets on the hips, patterned fabrics and drop waistlines – will all emphasize bottoms and hips.

If you wear skirts, do not fall for the common assumption that wide hips and a large bottom can be disguised by wearing long, full or A-line skirts. A well-cut, straight and slightly tapered skirt worn to the knee is much more flattering (see pp. 46-47). Also, avoid wearing skirts that cling too tightly – these will not be flattering if they look as if they are uncomfortable or the fabric is straining.

If you need a little bit of extra help, fabric technology means that we are no longer restricted to heavy corsetting. Look for bottom-enhancing, thigh-reducing and tummy-flattering briefs and hosiery. These are not necessarily the ugly passion-killers they once were.

### THICK THIGHS

Thick thighs should not be sheathed in clinging fabric worn with tight-fitting tops. This combination will make you look "bottom-heavy". Loose trousers and a gently shaped top that covers your

**FLATTERING FABRICS**

As a general rule, larger women should wear wool or natural fibres since these don't cling or give and, therefore, hold their shape better. However, ever-advancing fabric technology has resulted in some new fabric combinations that are extremely flattering on all sizes. The current favourite is a 96 percent wool, 4 percent Lycra combination. The most effective of these are bi-stretch fabrics (meaning they move laterally and vertically), which behave like an ordinary, solid wool until you actually move in them and feel the stretch. The fabric moves with the body but doesn't cling to it – perfect for camouflaging those bottom-half bumpy bits!

40

**Learning how to camouflage your hips and bottom is crucial – not only so that you can give the illusion of having a perfectly proportioned body but also for your own personal level of confidence.**

bottom are far more flattering. The thicker the fabric, the bigger your hips and thighs will look. Avoid fabrics, such as heavy tweeds or stiff linens, that may add unwanted bulk. Choose trousers and skirts made from fluid fabrics, such as lightweight wool, that can be worn all year round.  If you wear skirts or trousers that pull across the hip and thigh, you'll only accentuate the parts you'd rather minimize. It's better to opt for a larger size and then alter the garment to fit.

## THICK WAIST

If you have a thick waist, don't be fooled into thinking that wearing a belt will give you a waistline. It could have the reverse effect. Avoid clothes that are tight around the waist area. Clothes with a waist draw lines across the body, thereby accentuating a thick waist. Opt for styles that fall from the shoulders to a narrow hemline. Clothes that are gently shaped will create the illusion that you are more curvaceous than you are.

## WIDE, FLAT BOTTOMS

These are a more extreme form of the pear-shape and usually look better in a long jacket that will cover up and camouflage wide hips and large bottoms.

## NO HIPS, NO BOTTOM

If you are straight up and down, you may wish to try and create a more curvaceous effect. To do this, you will need to wear clothes that are fitted and may choose to wear a belt to draw attention to your waist. Also, jackets that are waisted and have details like peplums are flattering to a more boyish figure. If you are very slim as well, you may want to choose chunkier fabrics to add bulk to your frame. Remember that patterned fabrics add bulk, as do very bright colours such as red or orange.

**41**

### A MINUTE ON THE LIPS, FOREVER ON THE HIPS AND THIGHS

If you wish to stay slim, the best rule is not to indulge in an excess of anything. Remember that drinking plenty of water – between 3 and 5 litres (5 – 9 pints) a day is recommended. Eating a good diet, and exercising gently can make a huge difference to your shape, without requiring drastic action. We all know about cellulite and its causes but how many of us are prepared to give up the food that encourages the orange-peel effect? Body brushing using a good bristle brush, and stroking towards the heart will help encourage granulation. But in the end, diet and exercise are the only remedy.

# Legs & Feet

*As you age, your legs and feet need as much attention as your face. Of course, some women have a naturally better leg shape than others but with a little effort, everyone can improve the appearance of their legs.*

I always remember when my friend Joy and I were in Milan on a buying trip, we both noticed that, compared to ours, Italian women's legs seemed so much thinner. She quipped, "How do they get everything in theirs that we've got in ours?"

## CHOOSING YOUR CLOTHES TO MATCH YOUR LEGS

Those with perfect legs can wear any style of skirt or trousers. However, those who don't can easily flatter or worsen the shape of their legs by what they wear.

### THIN LEGS

Thin, bird-like legs can be just as restricting as chunkier legs when certain skirt-styles are fashionable. Very short skirts look wonderful on thin legs (age permitting) but skirts to the knee or just below the knee really don't work unless worn with thick, textured tights that add bulk to the leg. Trousers do not pose the same problem.

### BIG THIGHS

Straight trousers, with pleats, and loose on the thighs are the most flattering style. Trousers with a narrow hem accentuate the size of your thighs. Stick to straight, classic skirts as no extra bulk is needed.

### LARGE HIPS, THIN LEGS

Straight, slim-cut trousers and skirts will diminish the size of your hips and create the illusion that you are slim all over.

### CALVES

Thick calves are best hidden by wearing dark tights with a high Lycra content (about 14 percent). Those not wishing to wear opaque tights should opt for 20 denier in either barely black or mocha brown, which also disguise thick calves well.

## IMPROVING THE APPEARANCE OF YOUR LEGS

- Improve circulation by body brushing daily before bathing using a natural bristle brush in gentle sweeping movements towards the heart.

- Wear a shoe with a 3–4cm heel to add length to the leg, and improve calf muscle-tone.

- Exercise regularly to improve the shape of your leg.

- Camouflage scars or veins with blemish-cover cream.

- Wear high-cut swimsuits to give a longer and slimmer leg.

- Rest your legs, and avoid crossing them to discourage varicose veins.

- Massage moisturizer daily into the calves and thighs to improve circulation and skin condition.

- Rub a little baby oil into the knee area to soften the skin.

## CHUBBY OR KNOBBLY KNEES

Be aware that your hemline creates a horizontal line across the leg and will, therefore, draw attention to that part of the leg. If you hate your knees, then a hemline that stops just short of them will only add further emphasis.

**Often, when a woman has lost a lot of weight, there is one area where the fat stubbornly remains – her legs.**

## CHUNKY LEGS

Often, when a woman has lost a lot of weight, there is one area where the fat stubbornly remains – her legs. Very delicate shoes will only emphasize their chunkiness and narrow skirts with hemline details – pleats, for example – will draw further attention to them. Simple, straight skirts, to the knee, are best. Black or brown opaque tights (again with a high Lycra content) flatter the most. Try to create as sleek a line as possible by matching the colour of your shoes and your tights as this will make the leg look longer. Dark tights will make the leg look slimmer; lighter colours and bold patterns will have the opposite effect. Therefore, choose dark neutral-coloured shoes and dark tights. Remember: short skirts need good legs or legs that can be disguised with flattering hosiery.

## FEET

A common mistake that both women and men make is to neglect their feet. The feet take more weight and pressure than any other part of the body. Therefore, whether or not they spend most of the year hidden under socks, they deserve and need to be cared for. Shoes that don't fit can seriously damage your feet, even causing bunions, in which the bones of your feet change shape, which can be painful as well as unattractive.

If you have wide feet, they can be made more elegant by wearing shoes with a slightly elongated toe. Avoid high-cut shoes as these will make the foot look even wider.

Narrow feet can be more of a problem as the heel area of the shoe must grip the foot. A more closed-in style of shoe is often more comfortable for narrow feet. Some shoe manufacturers, such as Ferragamo, specialize in narrow fittings. This is an expensive make, but they will last and it is still cheaper than having your shoes made.

43

### FOOT CARE

● If you have wide feet buy shoes one size bigger and use a half inner sole to prevent them from being constricted should they swell up.

● Massage your feet regularly and alternate your shoes so that you are wearing different heel heights throughout the week.

● Visit a chiropodist twice yearly so that any potential problems can be detected and treated early.

● Cut your toenails regularly.

● When buying shoes with pointed toes, increase your shoe size by a half to prevent your feet from being pushed into the point, which is a common cause of bunions. If necessary use a half inner sole.

# Decisions

❖

*If you make a few, well-considered decisions before you add to your wardrobe you will have fewer problems (and no crises) to deal with in the future. A little forethought makes life so much easier!*

# Jackets

*The jacket is likely to be the most useful garment in your capsule wardrobe and, if chosen wisely, it will be an investment that will last for years. The right jacket may be expensive, but worth every penny.*

## BUYING A JACKET

● Look for simple shapes and clean, uncluttered lines. Your jacket will need to complement various shapes and styles of trousers, skirts and dresses.

● If you are buying a jacket to go with a skirt or trousers, remember that your jacket should always be of a matching or heavier fabric than that of your skirt or trousers. A light-weight jacket with a tweed skirt looks unattractive because the fabrics are out of proportion.

● Try on jackets using a three-way mirror so that you can clearly see what the back looks like.

● If you're buying a jacket made from a light-weight fabric, such as linen, allow for creasing, which will shorten the sleeves.

● If the sleeves of your jacket need to be shortened, buy a jacket where the buttonholes have not been cut through. If they have been cut, the sleeves will have to be shortened from the shoulder and this is a difficult tailoring job.

When I am asked if a jacket is really necessary for the workplace, I always reply "Absolutely". Jackets work wonders for your confidence and credibility. Quality *is* important though – while you may be able to get away with less expensive tops, trousers and skirts, the quality of fabric in a jacket is always obvious. And if it doesn't fit well, it will appear out of shape and do nothing to complement your figure. You should always buy the best jacket that your budget will allow. When buying your jacket ensure that there is enough room to wear a blouse or sweater underneath. Bring your arms forward across your chest to check that you are comfortable and that it is not too tight across the back. Can you move comfortably? Does the last button do up over your hips? If not, take a larger size and find a dressmaker to take it in at the back. This should be done at bust level for optimum comfort and fit.

**You should always buy the best jacket that your budget will allow.**

## Making your Choice

Extremes don't last in the world of fashion. Therefore, if you're on a budget or if you want to wear a jacket for more than one season, avoid bright colours and bold prints. Instead, buy jackets in neutral colours – black, navy, grey, beige or even sage green.

It is important to check how creased a garment is likely to become. A good test before purchasing a jacket is to scrunch up a section of fabric in your hand and hold it for five seconds. When you let go, certain fabrics will immediately fall back into shape. Others will appear creased and misshapen and no amount of smoothing the fabric will help.

46

**JACKETS** If chosen well, a jacket will show a high "cost-per-wear" return and is a good starting point in creating a new wardrobe. A jacket can help dress up or dress down an outfit and can be worn with trousers, skirts or even jeans for both day and evening wear. It is essential that a jacket fits well. The most important things to look for are shown here.

**COLLAR** This will vary in style. Ensure that it complements your shape and fits well with necklines of tops that you intend to wear underneath.

**FABRIC** If you intend to wear your jacket for most of the day, do not choose a loosely woven fabric. Instead, choose a stronger weave for durability.

**SHOULDER PADS** These should never reach beyond the width of your own shoulders unless you have very bulky arms (p.39). If you need extra padding, build upward not sideways.

47

**WAISTLINE** If the jacket is fitted, ensure that the darts are well stitched and do not pull around the waist.

**SLEEVE LENGTH** Your jacket should sit on or slightly below your wrist bone. If it has sleeve buttons ensure that there is at least a 2cm (1in) gap between the cuff and the first button.

**LINING** A good quality jacket will have a lining material in a colour that complements the fabric of the jacket.

**BUTTONS** Choose the number of buttons carefully. Large busts tend to bulge out of a single-button jacket. Opt for a two- or three-button style instead.

**HEMLINE** Always ensure that the left and right front panel of the jacket meet symmetrically at the hemline.

One word of warning: beware of chairs covered in abrasive fabrics (particularly in the work place where you may sit for several hours at a time) because the rough material can speed up the wear of your jacket.

## STYLE POINTS

Apart from general shape and fit, for example whether to buy a long or short, single or double-breasted jacket, there are other issues that you need to consider. These will help you to choose the right jacket for you.

### SHOULDER PADS

Since sizes increase and decrease with every new fashion season, my advice is to ignore the trends. Although deconstructed jackets are useful for informal occasions, most people need some form of padding.

48

**SINGLE-BREASTED JACKET**
This classic jacket is a good, first-purchase bet and is particularly flattering for women with larger busts. Styles range from several buttons to a single button.

**DOUBLE-BREASTED JACKET**
Extra fabric across the chest makes this a great style for disguising a smaller bust. Choose 2,4,6 or 8 buttons to suit your height and shape – the shorter you are, the fewer the buttons.

**LONG JACKET**
The longer length jacket does an excellent job in streamlining the figure as it falls well below the bottom. The longer your jacket, the narrower the trousers and shorter the skirt you wear with it should be. A long jacket worn with wide trousers or a long skirt will make you look shorter.

## BELTS

Belts are very flattering if you have slim hips, and they do show off a small waist. However, belted jackets accentuate the hips, and should therefore be avoided if this is an area you wish to disguise.

## BUTTONS AND BUTTON HOLES

Buttons are important and need to be considered carefully. Ensure that whatever you choose will be appropriate for both casual and formal occasions. It is no good buying a jacket with fancy buttons that preclude you from wearing it in the office.

## POCKETS

The style of pocket is an important consideration: large patch pockets or side vent pockets can bulk out the jacket and make you appear broader than you are, while stitched pockets can improve the line of your figure and help your jacket to retain its shape.

49

**COLLARLESS JACKET**
This is popular with women with large busts because the neckline is uncluttered and does not add bulk to the chest area. You need a slightly longer hair style to carry this type of jacket well because of the simplicity of the neckline.

**SHORT JACKET**
Short jackets are the most difficult shape to wear on their own and they tend to date faster than longer jackets. However, worn as part of a skirt-suit, they can look very feminine, especially for a more dressy occasion.

**RAGLAN SLEEVE JACKET**
The raglan sleeve feature gives the jacket a rounded shape. It is a very flattering style for women who have a good natural shoulder line, but is not so good for women with sloping shoulders as it provides no structure.

# Trousers

*Trousers are a great boon for both the career and non-career woman. Comfortable and easy to wear, they do not require heels and depending on your office environment, you may feel more at ease than in a skirt.*

You may not be accustomed to shopping with a tape measure in hand but the key to buying the right trouser is knowing the width of hem that suits your height and shape. Once you've measured a few, you'll be able to recognize "your" style of trouser at a glance and will be able to shop without the tape measure.

## TROUSER STYLES

There are many different cuts of trouser. Take the time to find the style that suits you best. The sizes quoted below are based on a size 10. They increase in direct proportion to an increase in trouser size.

### STRAIGHT OR TAPERED TROUSERS
*Hem width: 18–22cm*

Straight-legged or tapered trousers are consistent best-sellers because they are the most flattering style of trouser available. This is particularly true for shorter women who need to wear straight or slim-fitting styles in order to keep their overall proportions intact.

**Tip:** Those with bulky thighs should not be put off by tapered trousers. Just because they are tapered at the ankle doesn't mean they are tapered at thigh level too. If they fit on the thigh, they fit all over.

### CIGARETTE TROUSERS
*Hem width: 16–18cm*

Cigarette trousers are ultra narrow from thigh to ankle and, therefore, suitable for slim legs only.

### RELAXED TROUSERS
*Hem width: 22–26cm*

The relaxed or "slouch" trouser is long and often has front pleats and turn-ups. It is an easy style of trouser to wear but you need to be at least 5 ft 4in (1.63m) tall to carry it well. In the summer,

## CHOOSING THE RIGHT STYLE

● How do I know if a style of trouser really suits me?

● You can really feel it. Try on as many styles as possible using a triple-way mirror so that you can view the back of yourself easily. Quite often, trousers look great from the front but dreadful at the back. Don't be put off if the style you are trying on is far too long. You can always have the hem taken up. Do, however, be careful of taking up trousers that are tapered or flared. Shortening them excessively will alter the original shape.

however, shorter women can wear them as long as they are made from a fine fabric that moves with the body rather than simply covering it up.

   **Tip:** Looser trousers hide thicker thighs. But be careful not to go too loose – the trouser should still be a good fit around your bottom.

## CAPRI PANTS

This style comes in and out of fashion and suits all heights. Those with bulky thighs can wear capri pants (preferably with a top that covers your "derrière"), but you do need to have shapely calves and slim ankles since this area of the leg is exposed. Flat thong sandals complement this style although older women wishing to give maximum definition to their ankles and calves may wish to wear shoes with a slightly chunkier or wedge heel.

## THE DETAILS THAT MATTER

The criteria for a good trouser must be fabric, fit and finishings. Check the hip is put in well and works easily and that it fits well over your bottom. Check that the material is not too loosely woven.

## POCKETS

Trousers must fit well over the hip area, so the style of pockets is of great importance. Pockets cut on a slant are perfect for those who like to put their hands in their pockets. Vertical pockets, which look as though they have been sewn into the side seam of the trousers, are not ideal for wide-hipped women as they can bulge and gape.

   **Tip:** If you have bulky thighs and the lining of your pockets shows through the fabric of your trousers, ask a tailor to remove the pockets or, if you like to put your hands in your pockets, ask him to put in a thinner lining – fine silk is the ideal fabric.

## BELTS

If your trousers have belt loops, wear a belt. Otherwise it just looks as though you've forgotten to put one on. Always wear a belt that is about $1/5$ in ($1/2$ cm) narrower than the belt loops because if the belt matches the width of the loops exactly, the waistband may pucker and look ill-fitting. (For more information, see pp. 114–15.)

**RELAXED**
This is the largest trouser shape. It doesn't cling anywhere but fits well over the bottom. With or without turnups, it falls softly over the knee.

**CIGARETTE**
These are very narrow trousers from top to bottom. The hem finishes just above or just as the shoe starts. You need a thin pair of legs to wear them.

WAISTBANDS

As a rule, it is better to have a waistband than not. Although trousers without a waistband can create a "clean" and sleek silhouette on very slim women, on a woman with a slightly more rounded tummy, not having a waistband may accentuate excess flesh around the waist, whereas a waistband, like a belt, acts as a visual diversion.

Tip: Most women need to alter the waistbands of their trousers. It is worth doing, even if the alteration is minute, as it will affect the way the trouser hangs and the shape of the bottom.

## FABRIC

I would advise everyone to own a pair of straight, wool or wool-mix trousers as this classic style belongs in every capsule wardrobe.

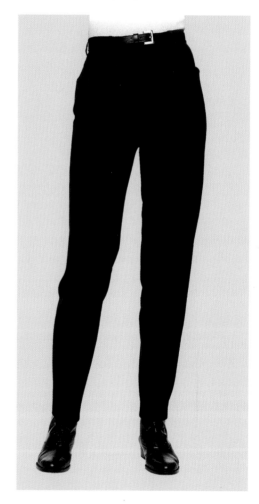

However, different styles lend themselves to different fabrics. Narrow trousers, for example, require a cloth with some stretch in it to stop the knee bagging, but a slightly wider-legged trouser doesn't need a stretch content so you can choose pure wool or a synthetic fabric. Body-revealing, fine fabrics, such as linen, should only be worn on narrow trousers if you are very slim. For more transparent, summer fabrics, choose a looser style.

## VISIBLE PANTY LINES

Visible panty lines look dreadful and can completely destroy the look of a beautiful pair of trousers. Try to get used to wearing G-strings instead of your usual underwear. If they seem uncomfortable, a bigger size usually helps.

**STRAIGHT**
This is the most classic shape and doesn't taper at the hem. It can be with or without pleats.

**TAPERED**
These are good for bigger hips and thighs as they taper towards the hem, slimming and elongating the leg. They look good worn with a chunky heel.

# Skirts

*Every time I'm asked what skirt lengths are "in" my response is always the same – "show me the legs I'm putting the skirt on." Forget fashion – think proportion.*

Skirt lengths and styles vary enormously and if you look, no single hemline is worn exclusively at any one time. My advice is to ignore the never-ending hemline debate and choose the skirt that suits your shape. However, if you wear a skirt that is too short into a business meeting, you risk being appreciated for your legs rather than your opinions.

**My advice is to ignore the never-ending hemline debate and choose the skirt which suits your shape.**

## FLATTERING SKIRTS

Regardless of style, a skirt must fit you properly if it is to look its best. Above all, it must fit over your hips. If it doesn't it will never hang properly. If you are one of the many women who has a small waist in proportion to your hips, as I've said before, it may be wiser to buy one size bigger and take in the waist.

### STRAIGHT OR TAPERED SKIRTS

If I could sell only one style of skirt, this would be it. A tapered skirt creates a flattering, streamlined look, although it should never be so narrow that it inhibits movement. Unlike other styles, it suits women of all ages, heights and shapes. On the knee is the best length unless you have very thin legs, in which case opt for a shorter or longer length instead. If you are larger on the hip area, your skirt can be tapered at the bottom only, therefore giving the illusion of narrowness without restricting movement. Variations of the straight skirt (those with back, front or side splits) can add interest and glamour to a classic garment.

### LONG SKIRTS

Although this style is unlikely to catch on as a suitable work-wear option, it can look very pretty in a light-weight fabric for summer, worn in a wrap or sarong style. I think long skirts, that is to say,

**TIPS**

● Despite the vertical lines of a pleated skirt – thought to have a slimming effect – pleats can add bulk. This is a risky shape to experiment with and I'd only recommend it to fashion experts.

● Long skirts can look good on young women. For older women they must be well cut and chic otherwise they can look frumpy.

from mid-calf to ankle-length, are more difficult to get right. I see many women, especially in summer, wearing long skirts to work (usually because they don't want to wear tights), which often look quite frumpy or more suitable for holiday wear. It can also be difficult to find a jacket that is the right shape for a long skirt, which, worn alone, can look rather messy. Long, shapely skirts can accentuate negative attributes and as I prefer to accentuate the positive ones, I am loath to recommend long skirts except for relaxed daywear. They are even more difficult in heavy fabrics because of added bulk, fluidity of shape is so essential. If you must wear long, buy the best you can afford because cut and cloth is crucial for a flattering fit.

CALF-LENGTH SKIRTS

Since the best part of many women's legs lies between her calf and ankle, these skirts can be very flattering. Personally, I prefer this shape tapered with a front, back or side split because it looks sexier.

## Skirts Styles to be Avoided

A-line skirts, very short skirts and pleated skirts all tend to be unflattering. The A-line style pulls the eye down, focusing on the body's lower half, and can easily look old-fashioned and matronly. And unless you are very young, with slim legs, avoid short flared skirts. Very short skirts are also best left alone since few women over 35 have knees good enough to expose. As for pleated skirts – keep away from them! Short pleated skirts look schoolgirlish and pleated skirts falling just below the knee look matronly.

## The Lining

Lined skirts are more comfortable to wear than unlined ones – they don't cling to tights, hang better and crease less. However, some skirts made from specific fabrics, such as double-face or stretch, are not meant to be lined and any skirt made from these fabrics would lose its style if it were lined. If you buy a skirt that does require lining, it is best lined with silk, if you can afford it, because this discourages static. If you buy an unlined skirt, ask the shop or a dressmaker to line it for you. Petticoats are made to a standard size and shape, which means they rarely "lie" well under a skirt.

**TAPERED**
This is the simplest skirt shape to wear. The length can be adjusted to suit the legs and the fashion. It looks good with most shoes.

**A-LINE**
This style is best on younger women as it can look matronly. It is not easy to wear with a jacket and is best worn with short tops. The most modern length is on the knee.

## FABRIC CONSIDERATIONS

When you are buying a skirt, especially if it is for work, you should consider how much time you spend sitting down and how often you move back and forth on your chair. If you swivel from your computer to your desk a lot, for example, a loose-weave fabric, such as some linens, will wear out quickly. It is, therefore, advisable to choose a closely-woven cloth, such as a pure wool gabardine, which doesn't wear or crease easily.

## SKIRT STYLES FOR THE OFFICE

Extremes in length are best avoided in business dressing. Long skirts can make you look dumpy and can be quite hazardous,

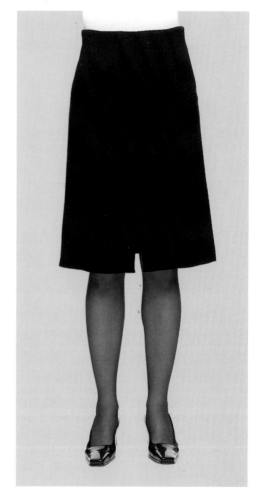

especially when walking up and down stairs, and a skirt that is too short might mean that you are taken less seriously than you deserve. Check how far your skirt rides up when you sit down and don't wear anything that is too revealing.

## SHOES AND SKIRTS

Choosing the right shoes for a skirt is all about getting the proportions right. In principle, the thicker the skirt's fabric, the heavier the shoe style, and vice versa. Hosiery is also instrumental in creating the right balance: fine evening skirts should be worn with fine denier tights just as wool skirts should be worn with heavier and possibly opaque tights depending on the fashion.

**MID-CALF**
This is a feminine shape for women with good calves and ankles. Sarongs are especially flattering at this length.

**LONG**
This is best for evening or casual daywear both in summer and winter. It is a difficult style to negotiate for daily use but looks good with chunky sweaters or, if you are a small size, slim-fitting tops that reach to your waist.

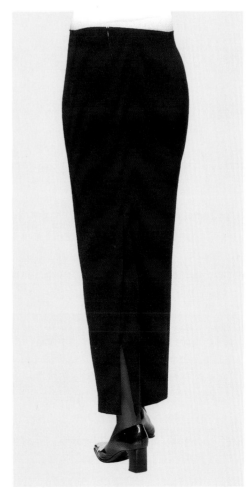

57

# Hosiery

*Hosiery says as much about a woman as her handbag or jewellery. The wrong hosiery can ruin a great outfit. When chosen well, it complements a chic and stylish garment.*

Hurray for Lycra! It's the fashion world's most important discovery this century. There is no doubt that tights with a Lycra content can improve the shape of the legs dramatically, so if your legs are less than perfect, take advantage of this wonder fabric and always look for tights with a high Lycra content.

## MATCHING TIGHTS AND SHOES

Many women make the mistake of matching the colour of their tights with the colour of the clothes they are wearing. It is far better to match them with your shoes, since this creates an unbroken line and the impression of a long, sleek leg. However, avoid matching brightly-coloured shoes with brightly-coloured tights.

**Tip:** It makes life much easier if you pack only brown and black shoes when travelling.

## WHAT TIGHTS WHEN?

In the summer or with evening-wear, wear fine, sheer 10-15 denier tights or stockings. When wearing natural shades in the summer, wear tights as close to your skin colour as possible, unless you have thick calves, in which case you should wear tights that are several shades darker than your skin tone. Beware of tan-coloured tights. Most of them have a reddish tint, which is unflattering to the leg.

During the winter, choose thicker, 20-60 denier tights. The denier should reflect the weight of the fabric from which your clothes are made. Clothes made from fine wool fabrics need thinner tights. Heavier fabrics need heavier tights. Personally, I find matt tights more flattering than shiny ones.

**MESH TIGHTS**
Fine mesh tights add interest to the leg without bulk – good for both young and mature women.

'*I keep seeing women wearing tights and open-toed shoes. It's dreadful – as bad as if I wore socks and sandals.* '

THOMAS KEENES, ART DIRECTOR

## WHAT TO WEAR UNDER TROUSERS

Tights fitted with a cotton gusset are good for wearing under slim-fit trousers because the in-built gusset negates the need for underwear and thus does away with any potential VPL problems.

Some women wear knee-high socks or pop sox, which, in my opinion, however well they serve their purpose, are one of fashion's ugliest inventions and the world's number one passion killer. If you do wear them, be sure to undress in private!

If, like me, you dislike pop sox and you don't want to wear tights, socks are the answer. Smart trouser socks are now available for women, which is good news since they look like socks as opposed to cut-off tights. Another bonus is that they don't mark the leg or resstrict circulation in the way that pop sox do. However, there is a great difference in quality between cheap and expensive socks. The less expensive ones tend to bag and wrinkle around the ankle, which will show when you sit down and your trousers ride up. It's worth buying socks with some Lycra content, which will help to keep them in place.

**There is no doubt that tights with a Lycra content can improve the shape of the legs dramatically**

**Tip:** Remember that if you're going to wear a dress or skirt after a day in trousers, roll down your socks or knee-highs in time for the markings from the elastic to disappear from your legs (as you get older, it takes longer for the marks to go!)

## WEARING TIGHTS TO WORK

I would advise most women to wear tights to work, even in summer – after all, you don't see men walking into the office without their socks on. Most hosiery manufacturers now produce very fine tights, which are more comfortable to wear in the heat. However, if temperatures soar and the idea of wearing tights is unbearable, wear

59

a trouser suit with open-toe shoes – just make sure your toe nails are pedicured, polished and pretty enough to expose.

Tip: After you have dressed, always look in a full-length mirror. Often you will find the beginnings of a ladder at the back of your leg that you missed when putting your tights. Always keep a spare pair of tights in your handbag, desk drawer or car glove compartment. There's nothing worse than going to a meeting with a ladder in your tights.

## A Word on Wearing Stockings

Don't wear suspenders with fine evening fabrics such as satin and silk. They will show through the fabric and spoil the look of your outfit. Hold–ups are a safer bet, though they can be uncomfortable and leave marks on your thighs.

**WHAT DENIER TO WEAR**
In the summer choose 5–15 denier, although be aware that these are the most delicate tights. 15–40 denier are suitable for most winter styles in normal winter-weight wool. If you are wearing a thicker fabric, go for 20–60 denier, which are increasingly opaque.

60

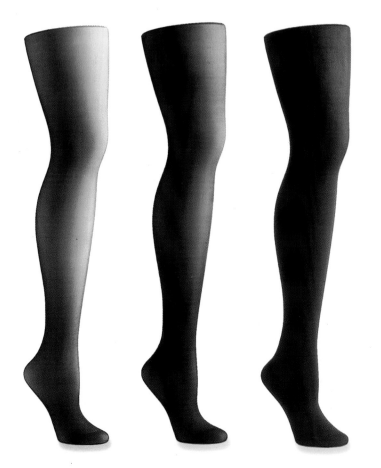

Always keep a spare pair of tights in your handbag, desk drawer or car glove compartment. There's nothing worse than going to a meeting with a ladder in your tights.

## WONDERBRAS FOR BOTTOMS

Strange but true! There are tights that literally "lift" the bottom. Great for those whose bottom halves are not as toned as they'd like them to be, these tights give a smooth and flattering line, particularly under slinky evening dresses. However, they are often a struggle to put on and remove and are generally not the prettiest hosiery designs available – like pop sox, they leave marks on your skin and should be removed in private. If you are worried about your stomach as well, there are tights that have a panel at the front to pull you in a bit. But do make sure that they are comfortable before wearing them for a whole day or evening.

## COLOURED AND PATTERNED HOSIERY

I have a problem with coloured hosiery. Although it can be a fun way for younger women to accessorize an outfit, it often makes women stand out, in the wrong kind of way, and can even make you look older than your years. Even navy tights rarely look good and can be ageing. If you wear navy shoes, match them with barely black tights instead.

With brown shoes, wear brown or natural-coloured tights, black or barely black tights with black shoes or, if fashion dictates (and your legs are good), a pair of good quality, natural-coloured tights.

Hosiery trends change frequently. Keep up with what's on offer without sacrificing your own good taste. White tights may be all the rage on the catwalk but the question to ask is, will they look good on you?

Lacy or patterned tights and stockings draw attention to your legs and have a nasty habit of looking like varicose veins from a distance. However, a very fine mesh can do wonders if light-coloured tights are in fashion and your legs are less than perfect (I speak from personal experience).

When you buy an outfit, your tights are a very important accessory. It is worth spending time getting the colour and denier right. Tights are really like makeup for your legs and your legs are quite a large area of your body to cover. I find going to a specialist hosiery shop is a worthwhile time investment – especially if you end up buying a cheaper brand.

### HOW TO MAKE YOUR TIGHTS LAST

We've all experienced the frustration of opening a fresh packet of tights only to snag them a few seconds later. Here's how to keep your hosiery ladder-free.

● You get what you pay for. Buy the best hosiery you can afford. If you're unsure of which brand to buy, ask the hosiery sales assistant of a reputable department store which label she recommends.

● One Size never fits all. Buy brands that sell different sizes so that you can achieve a sheer, second-skin look from a really well-fitting pair of tights. Buy them too small and they'll ladder easily, buy them too big and they will bag around your ankles.

● Before putting on your tights make sure that your fingernails are filed until smooth. Put on some hand cream to get rid of any rough skin. Put a dab on your feet too as they get very dry, particularly in the winter. Use a pumice stone on big toes and heels daily as this is where hard skin collects most – the harder your skin the easier it will be to snag your tights.

● Don't keep tights in a drawer with sharp edges. I keep mine in shoeboxes – a convenient way to store them and one that prevents tights from catching. Store them according to colour for quicker choice.

61

# Lingerie

*How many of us think about our underwear without remembering those famous words of caution, "Always wear nice underwear, dear. If a bus runs you down, you don't want to be discovered wearing old undies!"*

However silly, this tale has me, (and many others) unable to wear mismatching underwear. There is something about beautiful underwear that makes a woman feel incredibly good. In fact, many women I have spoken to have said that in times of crisis, such as divorce or separation, they went out and had an underwear binge and felt better for it.

As I mention in The Capsule Wardrobe (see pp. 72–83), good lingerie that fits is the basis of an effective wardrobe. There is an enormous range available now, from feminine, lacy French briefs and camisoles to very sporty, simple cotton briefs and vests. Lingerie should be comfortable and make you feel good. It is also important that it enhances whatever you are wearing over it, as superb clothes can easily be ruined by ill-fitting lingerie underneath.

**Tip:** Never put good-quality lingerie in a washing machine. The spinning action of the drum in the machine will distort the shape and may damage any wiring. Wash your underwear by hand using a mild detergent instead.

### FABRIC

Silk is without rival for glamour and sensuality. Silky underwear is an extravagance, albeit a delicious one, but natural fibres will need ironing, whereas polyester does not. I think that every woman ought to have the indulgence of one set of silk underwear or pyjamas, which are my personal preference. The sensation of silk against the skin is wonderful and makes you feel pampered.

If you buy lined skirts then petticoats will be

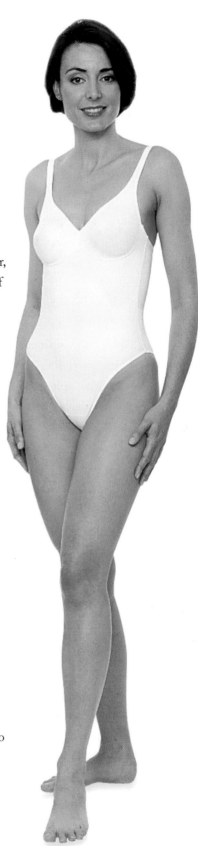

‘ *Without foundations,
there can be no fashion.* ,

CHRISTIAN DIOR, FASHION DESIGNER

redundant in your wardrobe. However, if you have a need for a
slip, then a straight one without detail is best, worn literally as an
"underskirt" with the same fitting considerations that apply to the
skirt itself (see pp. 54–57).

Specialist underwear, such as sports bras and thermal underwear,
can be vital in certain circumstances. A vast range of these types of
garment is available, so I would urge shopping around to find
exactly what you're looking for.

For the times when you want to put the day behind you and
relax, I find one of the most useful pieces of lingerie is a dressing
gown, in a fabric that either feels very cosy, like towelling and
superfine cottons, or something more sensual like silk or
cashmere. Just the thing to slip into after a hard day in the
office and a long soak in the bath. Enjoy!

## COLOUR

It is vital to think about the colour of your top layers when
buying underwear, since it can show through, especially at the
height of the summer when many of us wear lightweight fabrics
in pale colours. If you don't want to have to bother to think
about this, then invest in some flesh-coloured lingerie. There
are many different shades of nude available to suit every
skin tone.

## ALL-IN-ONE "BODIES"

For a very smooth line, a body – an all-in-one undergarment,
almost like a swimsuit – is very comfortable. These do up under
the crotch and it is important, for the sake of comfort, that they do
up with large poppers instead of buttons or hooks and eyes. They
are perfect for wearing under knitted clothes or cotton jersey, will
keep you warm and are much sexier than thermal underwear!

63

64

## BRAS

Amazingly, seven out of ten women do not wear the correct size of bra. I always advise trying a bra before you buy it and many specialist shops offer a free measuring service. If you cannot locate one, here are some easy guidelines on how to measure yourself.

To measure yourself you need your back size, which relates to your body size and is represented by a number (e.g. 34, 36, 38), and your cup size, represented by a letter, A, B, C etc.

• To find your bra back size, measure in inches around your body under your bust. Pull the tape measure as tight as your bra strap would be, snug but not uncomfortable. This will save you wearing a back size that is too big – one of the most common mistakes.

• You won't need a tape measure to find the right cup size. Your breasts should be fully enclosed by the cup, unless you are wearing a half-cup bra style. If a cup is too big, there will be excess fabric. If too small, you will bulge over. Do remember that breast shapes, like body shapes, vary, and one woman's 34-inch bust can be very different from another's. Wearing the wrong size can be both painful and damaging to your shape. It is worth the effort to get it right. If you have a large bust, make sure that the cup size is adequate because the cups provide most of the support. You may feel most secure in an underwired bra, although be sure that the wiring is

**MATCHING UNDERWEAR**
Many ranges of underwear
are designed in several styles
but in the same fabrics and in
all colours so that you can mix
and match to your heart's
content. Soft bras, far left,
are comfortable and easy to
wear for women who do not
have a large bust. Underwired
bras, left, are more suitable
for the fuller figure. Styles of
briefs vary – high briefs hide
your stomach and pull it in
more than styles that are cut
low. There are also many
designed with panels in the
front that pull in and flatter
your stomach (left). Neutral
colours are the most versatile
and can be worn under
everything but dark, thin,
clothing. Many people prefer
to wear dark underwear under
dark clothes.

comfortable. Straps should be wide enough to not cut into you, and
to avoid bulges forming above the cups or under the arms.
Fortunately, for larger women, bras are now made to fit under every
style of clothing, even backless dresses.

## BRIEFS

Briefs should fit snugly, otherwise ugly lines will show through your
clothing. If you think you need some support over your stomach
area, wear tights or briefs with a control panel at the
front. Wearing tights with a cotton gusset prevents the
dreaded VPL (visible panty line) under tight skirts or
trousers because you won't need briefs as well. If you find
G-strings comfortable, they also help create a smooth
line. There are many different styles of G-string on the
market now – only wear those that feel comfortable. (The true test
of comfortable underwear is to feel as though you're not wearing
any at all.) Lacy underwear, including French briefs, although very
pretty, can be too bulky to wear under close-fitting clothes. Save
them for wearing with looser garments.

Tip: To flatter your stomach to the maximum, buy briefs and
G-strings that reach above the navel. The lower they are cut, the
higher the risk of tummy overflow!

Fortunately, for larger women,
bras are now made to fit under
every style of clothing ...

# Makeover *Sally*

A lthough Sally works from home, her job involves regular meetings with publishers, magazine editors and celebrities whom she sometimes interviews. She asked us to help her achieve a modern look, while bearing in mind that she is a grandmother.

## BEFORE

Sally was not making the most of a pretty face and a good figure. Like many women in their mid-50s, she has lost the confidence to experiment and has been wearing comfortable clothes, without giving much thought to style. She was also worried that she might end up looking like "mutton dressed as lamb". Her hair was beginning to fade from its natural, rich red and the original style was too square and was growing out. The shirt and sweater that Sally was wearing did not work well with the V-neck of the shirt and left areas under the lapels visible. Moreover, since the colours contrasted so sharply, attention was drawn to a block of neck, shoulders, jawline and hair. As a result, this area looked quite bulky, the outline of her hair visually linking the line of her shoulders and upper arms, making Sally's neck look short.

**Each item chosen here is versatile and crease-resistant**

## WHAT WE DECIDED TO DO

It wasn't going to be hard to make Sally look her best as she was still an attractive woman and had kept her figure. We wanted to aim at a comfortable but chic, dignified style that would travel well. Although Sally's work allows a fairly informal approach to her clothes, we thought that although her trousers looked very nice, a matching skirt and top would be more elegant. (Turn to p. 68.)

66

### VITAL STATISTICS

Sally Chater
**Age:** Mid-50s
**Height:** 5ft 5in
**Dress size:** 14
**Occupation:** Freelance writer
**Aim:** To project a style which is contemporary, versatile, relaxed and comfortable to travel in, while remaining businesslike.

' *I felt absolutely great – stylish, sexy and ten years younger!* '
SALLY

**JACKET** This casual jacket/shirt is ideal for informal day or business wear. The unstructured shape and soft, luxurious suede fabric make the garment extremely comfortable and easy to wear, as well hard-wearing and crease-resistant.

**COLLAR** The soft suede collar falls gently away from the neck, and distracts attention from an area Sally didn't want to be prominent.

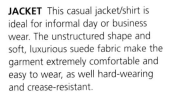

**FABRIC** The use of suede need not be limited to heavy, lined garments. It can also be light and soft, as this jacket shows. The fluid lines and tactile texture make this a very versatile item for either smart or casual wear.

**TWO PIECE** The knitted, wool two-piece is especially good for travelling as it won't crease. It makes the most of Sally's figure without clinging, and set against the jacket, the colour is very flattering. It is also a dateless outfit.

**BAG** As Sally's lifestyle involves lots of travelling around town, she needs a good-sized bag for all her necessities. This classic leather bag is the ideal proportion for Sally's needs and her outfit. The leather is hard-wearing, and works well with the suede jacket and shoes. A suede bag would be too much!

**SHOES** Either the wedge sandal worn here, or a flat leather mocassin, work well with this mid-calf length, wool skirt. To maintain the right proportions of fabric textures, a heavier denier of tights were chosen.

67

Trousers are stylish for older women, but there is no need to forget that they have legs too, and in Sally's case, very nice ones! We needed to unclutter her neckline and to cut her hair to make her neck look longer. We also decided to colour it with a tone that reflected her original colour and would complement her skin.

### CLOTHES

We dressed Sally in a dark, knitted two-piece that could be worn separately with ease (the sweater with trousers, the skirt with another top or shirt). Note the rounded and gently scooped neckline of the sweater, deliberately chosen to flatter her neck. We chose a dark colour as it suited Sally's complexion and hair, and is very slimming. We also thought that for meetings it was both fashionable and sophisticated. The wool skirt came to mid-calf, which is a very flattering length, particularly on tall women, and tapered very slightly towards the bottom, flattering Sally's legs and ankles. Dark tights with dark shoes accessorized the outfit well. The wedge-heeled suede shoes were stylish but comfortable for travelling to and from meetings. To complete the look, we chose a suede shirt jacket

## By layering her hair, we were able to lift it away from the face making her look younger.

' *Foundation is the key to evening out your skin tone and concealing small imperfections. This is why it is vital that you find the right colour and formula for your skin.* '

MAGGIE HUNT, MAKE-UP ARTIST

that Sally could wear with skirts, trousers or dresses. The cut fills out her shoulder line, which helps to disguise her own sloping shoulders.

Since Sally travels regularly, comfort and practicality were of particular importance. Each item chosen was versatile and crease-resistant. The wedge shoes we chose could easily be replaced by a pair of flat moccasins for a sportier look.

## HAIR

Sally's short, square bob didn't flatter her square face. By layering her hair, we lifted it away from her face making her look younger, and created a rounded, voluminous style. Reducing the amount of hair directly above her shoulders also flattered her neck. Simply by adding some more red to Sally's naturally red hair colour, we managed to create the illusion of a "lifted", brighter complexion.

## MAKE-UP

We wanted to enhance rather than alter Sally's features so we applied a slightly darker tone along her jawline to soften it and brightened the colour of her skin tone with lipstick and blusher.

### OLDER COMPLEXIONS

Your make-up should change as you grow older, in the same way that your style of clothing should change. If you use the same make-up as you did ten years ago, not only will it look dated but it will no longer suit your complexion. As you age, the skin becomes drier, lines appear and your lips will be less well-defined. But don't lose heart! Help is at hand.

Here are a few dos and don'ts that apply specifically to caring for the older complexion. I have found them very helpful.

● The heavier the foundation, the more obvious wrinkles appear. Use a light foundation or tinted moisturiser that matches the neck so that the tone blends invisibly with the chin and jawline.

● Use a little translucent or light-diffusing powder to remove shine.

● Shimmery eyeshadow emphasises lines or crepeyness on the lids. Avoid strong colours. Soft, muted neutrals, such as greys or browns, are best.

● Mascara and eye-pencil have a definite role to play, but blend them in gently to define your eyes. Avoid harsh lines around the eyes.

● Creamy-textured lipsticks in mid-tones are the most flattering on older women.

● Put lipstick on *first*. Then use a pencil to outline your lips.

# Cut, Cloth, Colour

❖

*Always buy the best that you can afford. Quality shows and lasts longer, which, over time, is more cost-effective. Buy basic items in neutral colours and you will have a stylish, co-ordinating wardrobe with endless possiblities.*

# Capsule Wardrobe

*Believe it or not, despite having access to a whole shop full of clothes, I have a very concise wardrobe. It's heaven! Having a capsule wardrobe makes perfect sense – in terms of both style and space!*

Few people I know need vast amounts of clothes in order to either look or feel confident and well-dressed. I like to have clothes that work from morning until night and I only like to wear clothes of good quality, which means that I can't have a lot of them. Therefore, I need clothes that have different lives – suits that can be split apart, a jacket that can be dressed from day to evening and even put with jeans on the weekend – and so on.

What I am advocating in this chapter – and throughout the book – is that you reduce rather than increase the number of clothes in your wardrobe. Instead of having lots of clothes, many of which are hardly worn, I'd like to help you own a smaller number of clothes from which you will get greater wear – the ultimate "less is more" philosophy.

### WHERE DO I BEGIN?

Apply the Three Piles Principle (see p. 99) and take photographs of the clothes that you own and like. When you go shopping, take these pictures with you to remind yourself of the cut and colour, thus ensuring that what you buy will complement what you already have.

### WON'T I GET BORED?

OK, now let's deal with safe and boring. The thought of having so few clothes worries many women and one of the questions I'm asked most frequently is, "But won't I get bored wearing the same clothes all the time?" The answer is no. Having a capsule wardrobe is liberating. It is a great way of clearing your mind and helping you to focus. Boredom doesn't enter the equation because the whole point of a capsule wardrobe is that it provides you with a variety of choices. It also takes away the possibility of making expensive mistakes in the future. If you do feel bored with your clothes, the

**Having a capsule wardrobe is liberating. It is a great way of clearing your mind and helping you to focus.**

### COLOUR-CODING

Trends don't last in the world of fashion and this applies not only to cut but also to colour. Your capsule wardrobe should be made up of monochrome neutrals: black, navy, beige, greys, browns, white, greens and ivory. You can start to play with colour once your capsule wardrobe is in order. If you really want to add colour to your capsule wardrobe do it with your blouse, your sweater, a scarf or even a new lipstick.

72

*' You don't have to spend a fortune to look good – just prioritize essentials that'll blow the budget and make savings elsewhere '*

LIZZIE RADFORD, LAWYER

chances are that you've made wardrobe mistakes in the past! So resist the temptation to rush off and buy new clothes. Buy some new make-up or change your hairstyle instead. It's a lot cheaper!

## HOW LONG WILL IT LAST?

If chosen well, a capsule wardrobe should last for four to five years. But remember that it is only the foundation upon which you will build the rest of your wardrobe. I like to use the following analogy. Imagine that the capsule wardrobe is your "family" and that the bits and pieces that make up the rest of your wardrobe are your "friends". If you choose your friends wisely, they'll fit in with the family and hopefully become friends of the family for a very long time!

Once you've bought your basic capsule wardrobe you can start to add to it each season. If money is no object you may decide to have a new capsule wardrobe every six months – although this is very rare. What I advise most women to do is to buy a fashionable garment each season that will fit in with their existing capsule wardrobe, a skirt, for example, to go with a jacket bought the year before. Keep on adding and then when your original capsule wardrobe is perhaps four or five years old you can think of discarding some of the original pieces.

## THE DEFINITIVE CAPSULE WARDROBE

A capsule wardrobe is a small, considered collection of clothes that provides an effective minimum number of garments to meet your daily needs. It is the solid foundation upon which to build the rest of your wardrobe. The "capsule" centres on a jacket and includes a skirt, trousers (which could be part of a suit), a blouse, a sweater, shoes, tights, underwear, a coat or raincoat, a dress, a bag, a belt, jewellery, gloves and evening wear. If chosen wisely, these pieces,

## TIPS

● The success of the capsule wardrobe depends very much on the choice of jacket cloth. It should be chosen to fit in with several "bottom-halves" – skirts and trousers. If you opt for a pattern rather than plain cloth, be sure it is unobtrusive. Discreet patterns, small checks and stripes can work well. Bear in mind clothes that you already own. For example, if you possess a grey skirt and black trousers, a pattern that incorporates these two colours and one other will work very well. With the addition of a couple of blouses and a sweater, the jacket can now be worn in six outfit combinations. (If, however, your first purchase is a suit – either a jacket and skirt or jacket and trousers – you don't necessarily need to look for a textured cloth as the two pieces will match anyway.)

● Choose colours with longevity in mind. Muted colours – navy, grey, brown and beige – are best as they are timeless and essentially immune to changes in fashion. You might think you look terrific in bright red but you are buying your jacket for maximum wear. Furthermore, the colours in your jacket provide the basic colours in your capsule wardrobe.

73

in many combinations, will provide an outfit for every occasion. Never again should you be faced with a wardrobe overflowing with clothes and the dilemma of "what on earth shall I wear?"

Below is a list of the items, listed in descending order of importance, that will form the basis of your capsule wardrobe.

### JACKET

The jacket is by far the most important, and most versatile, item in a capsule wardrobe. This is the one garment to really splash out on. If chosen well, a jacket will show a high "cost-per-wear" return and is your wisest starting point. (For guidelines on jacket styles see pp. 46-49).

Once you've found the shape of the jacket that is right for you, you should look at the fabric. A textured cloth in a plain colour is the most versatile because when it is worn with trousers or a skirt, it won't matter if the colours don't match exactly, as the different textures will make it obvious that you are wearing two individual pieces, not a suit.

### SKIRT

A straight skirt, tapered to the knee or fractionally below, is your best bet. Look for those made from a cool wool or light-weight gabardine as these will take you through most of the year. Make sure that there is no detailing that will conflict with the buttoning of your jacket. (For example a front-split skirt will look imbalanced with the line created by a double-breasted jacket).

The colour of your skirt should be compatible with that of the jacket. A large block of bright colour will only draw undesirable attention to your lower half, which may not be your best point. A muted colour, either matching the jacket or picking out an accent

**Make sure that there is no detailing that will conflict with the buttoning of your jacket.**

colour from the jacket, will look far more attractive. If you choose a skirt in the same colour as your jacket buy it in a textured fabric if the jacket is a smooth fabric or vice versa. This eliminates the problem of dyes of the same colour varying.

## TROUSERS

Look for straight trousers that are neither too wide nor too narrow. These suit most jacket shapes – either short or long – and most shoe styles as well. The most useful trousers will be those that you can wear during the day and evening. (A useful test is to try the trousers on with smart day shoes and strappy sandals. If the trousers suit both, you're on to a winner!) If you're investing in one pair of trousers I would advise you to buy those made from either pure wool gabardine or those with a 96% wool, 4% Lycra content.

Note: Trousers are made up from relatively narrow pieces of cloth and they cover a large area of the body, so large patterns and bright colours will draw the eye to the trousers rather than the person inside them. Stick to monochrome colours instead. As I am writing this, I'm beginning to smile – I can hear you, the reader, asking "Isn't this all a bit safe and boring?" Hold on to that thought, I'll return to it soon.

## SWEATER

The simpler the sweater, the better. Choose styles with a round neck and short sleeves (long sleeves are fine if you feel the cold). Fine fabrics such as Merino wool, wool and silk mix or cashmere, if your budget permits, are best, since heavy fabrics are uncomfortable and can look too bulky when worn under jackets.

As with blouses, this is the time when you can have some fun with colour. Choose either a sweater that is the same tone as your suit or a contrasting pastel colour such as pale blue or pink. Successful combinations are a mint-green or powder-blue sweater under a sage-green suit, a sky-blue sweater under a navy or brown suit or a pale pink sweater under a grey or brown suit.

## COAT

A coat is likely to be an investment, a "major purchase" that you will use for several years. Always choose a long coat

### CHOOSING A BLOUSE

In terms of dressing for business, your blouse (or sweater) is the equivalent of a man's tie. It is the garment that can bring colour and life to an outfit and that you will change frequently. You will probably change your blouse every day so you are likely to own several different ones. To begin with, allow yourself a minimum of two. Those with cutaway or men's style collars are easy to wear under jackets but they can look quite masculine. Counteract this by unbuttoning the top two buttons and perhaps adding a scarf to soften the hard lines. Remember, a softly tailored blouse, sweater or top can take your suit from day to evening wear.

75

(mid-calf or longer) since these will look stylish no matter what fashion dictates. The shape and length of your coat will depend on your height – the smaller you are, the more fitted a long coat should be. Although it may seem obvious, it is essential that you hold up a long coat, as you would a long evening dress, when going up and down stairs to avoid catching your heels in the hem, and either tripping up or pulling the hem down. A long coat will also keep you warm, which is particularly important if this is the only coat that you have. It needs to be roomy enough to sit comfortably over a suit, yet not so large that it looks ridiculous if you slip it over a dress in the evening.

To get the maximum wear, buy your coat in black or dark grey – practical colours suitable for both daytime and evening wear. A cream or honey-coloured coat may look stunning but it is a "feel-good" luxury. But if you really want to spoil yourself, go for it!

The best fabrics for coats are either wool, wool and angora, wool and cashmere or, budget-permitting, pure cashmere. However, looking at the fabric content on a label is not enough. There are many coat fabrics that feel warm to the touch but, when faced with a freezing chill, allow the wind to pass straight through them. My advice is to buy your coat on a cold day and to try it on outside.

> *If you have a stylish coat that suits you, you will feel confident entering any place, anywhere*
>
> HILARY BROOKS
> PR ACCOUNTS MANAGER

**To get the maximum wear from your coat, buy it in black or dark grey – practical colours suitable for both daytime and evening wear.**

## RAINCOAT

Having a coat and a raincoat is ideal but if your budget is limited, a good quality, just-below-the-knee raincoat that can be worn all year round should suffice. Again a neutral colour – black or stone – is most useful. A raincoat should be generously cut so that you can wear your heaviest suit under it comfortably. Raincoats are also very useful travelling companions so don't buy one that is too heavy. Many are made with belts, but the belt does not always need to be worn for the coat to look good. Remember that if you choose a raincoat that needs a belt, and you are wearing several layers underneath, you run the risk of looking bulky and bundled-up around the middle when you tighten the belt.

A raincoat should protect you from the wind, as well as the rain. Lots of flaps, deep slits and openings in the design will not do this. Choose a smoothly constructed raincoat. If in doubt, choose a well-established manufacturer. These may be more expensive than other designs but they will last several years. Those made with a detachable lining are particularly useful for year-round comfort.

## DRESS

The dress in your capsule wardrobe should be as simple as possible. Straight, knee-length shift styles in black or navy are the most useful. Choose from sleeveless, cap-sleeved or elbow-length sleeves depending on how comfortable you feel about revealing your upper arms (bulky sleeves and trims will not sit well under a jacket). The ideal neckline sits approximately 3cm (1in) below the collarbone – both modest enough for daytime amd office wear but low enough for jewellery to be worn in the evening. Choose the dress in a fabric most suited to your lifestyle: a pure wool or wool, stretch fabric if you are likely to get most wear from your dress during the day or a wool crepe or synthetic jersey crepe (one that doesn't cling) if you wish to wear it regularly in the evenings.

## SHOES

You will need at least two pairs of shoes, a black pair and a brown pair, or depending on the colour of your clothes, possibly two black pairs. Buy one pair with a slightly chunky heel to wear with trousers and the other with a more delicate heel for wearing with skirts and in the evening with skirts or trousers. Good quality leather is best – suede looks softer but needs more care.

## TIGHTS

You should have at least three pairs of tights in your wardrobe at all times: one black, one sheer black or nearly black and one natural brown. For more on tights see pp. 58–61 (Continued on p.80).

> ' *Shoes are a much more important accessory than many people think, particularly if you call on clients a lot. In the visitor's chair, they attract a lot of attention.* '
>
> JANE COOPER. SENIOR MANAGER, BANKING

## WORKING WOMEN

Working women need to combine comfort with a stylish, usually tailored, look so that they are dressed to the same level as, (or better than) their male peers. A suit is the most versatile garment and can be worn on all occasions. When choosing your suit, consider carefully what you do during the day – if you sit a lot, for example, the material will require more "give" than if you stand most of the time.

**JACKET** A grey jacket can be teamed with various skirts or trousers. Jackets can be taken off when it's warm or for a less formal look.

**SKIRT** A knee-length skirt in a light material is elegant, and the length ensures it doesn't ride too far up your thighs when you sit down.

**TROUSERS** Trousers are very comfortable office wear. A pair that matches your jacket creates a whole new look and can be worn with the same choice of tops and shoes as the suit skirt.

**SUIT FABRIC** Light-weight wool is suitable for office wear – light enough for indoor wear and pliant enough to be comfortable when you sit at a desk.

**EVENING SHOES** Heels elongate the leg and can be worn with either a skirt or trouser suit, provided that the trouser legs are not too narrow.

**DAY SHOES** Court shoes with a lowish heel are elegant, understated and, just as importantly, comfortable for everyday wear.

78

**V-NECK** A V-neck is an attractive neckline, which does not need to be jazzed up with a scarf. A scarf is also a hazard for women who deal with young children regularly.

## NON-CAREER WOMEN

Non-career women will have as many criteria to consider as the working ones but are more likely to be in a position to wear looser, less closely constructed clothes. Comfort, as ever, must be paramount. Depending on their lifestyle, they may require uncluttered, "baby-proof" clothing that is easy to wash and needs little or no ironing. Clothes made from stretch fabrics may be a consideration – allowing them to pick up children, shopping bags or to drive comfortably. For this more physically strenuous lifestyle, trousers may be more convenient, allowing greater fluidity of movement and the opportunity to wear flatter, more solid shoes or boots.

**79**

**CARDIGAN** A cardigan over a matching top is a versatile, smart item, acting in much the same way as a jacket for the working woman. Soft fabric allows fluid movement and the sleeves can be pushed up easily out of the way.

**TROUSER FABRIC** If you love the feel of a pair of trousers and the way the fabric falls, plus it has easy washing instructions, you will live in your trousers. Soft fabrics with some "give" in them are especially comfortable.

**TROUSERS** The length and width of your trousers will depend on your own personal preference, but wider trousers will be looser, airier and more comfortable.

**SHOES** Chunky, flat shoes look great with trousers and are comfortable to wear – especially necessary if you are on your feet all day, running around.

## JEWELLERY

Jewellery is an intensely personal accessory and this is where your own preferences should come into play. However, boldly coloured and chunky jewellery doesn't belong in your capsule wardrobe. Instead, choose discreet styles. Two pairs of earrings are enough: one pair of pearl studs since the way they reflect onto the face lights up every complexion, and one pair of small, gold hoop or small stud earrings. If you're desperate to incorporate some colour, choose some earrings with a coloured central stone, but these will be limited in terms of what you can wear with them.

> Jewellery is an intensely personal accessory and this is where your own preferences should come into play.

## SCARF

Scarves are a blessing! By placing a scarf around the neckline of your jacket you can save yourself a fortune in dry-cleaning bills since a jacket accumulates most dirt from make-up around the collar. Even if you don't wish to wear a scarf all day, wearing one for the first hour of the day helps enormously, as this is when most of your make-up will come off. (And, of course, scarves are much cheaper to clean than jackets.)

Scarves are also your chance to play with colour. Keep a selection of prints and patterns that pick out the colours of the rest of your capsule wardrobe. Choose square or oblong scarves depending on the collar of the garments you're accessorizing (For more on scarves, see pp. 122–23).

## BAG

For working women, a brown or black leather bag that doubles up as a brief-case is best. Those styles fitted with a shoulder strap and two handles are best as they can prevent back ache. I make a point of carrying a stylish leather make-up bag into which I can put my purse, keys, mobile phone and money, should I wish to nip out of the office without carrying my large bag. (Continued on p. 83.)

### UNDERWEAR

Frills, bows and lace trimming are fine for special occasions but they don't belong in your capsule wardrobe. What does are simple, seam-free bras and matching smooth-line briefs and G-strings. Three basic colours are all you need: black, white and nude for wearing under white and pale colours.

## GRADUATE WOMEN

Recently graduated from university, Graduate Women will be in either a formal office environment and should follow the guidelines for Career Women, or in a less formal office where the dress code is more casual. In a less formal, possibly small office, they may be required to do a variety of jobs – desk and non-desk based – and will require a versatile outfit to cover their varied day. However, they should not be tempted to give their appearance little thought – even if it seems acceptable – the psychology of appearance still applies and they will be taken more seriously if they look casual-smart.

**TOP** A white T-shirt or shirt is trendy and looks stylish with virtually any plain colour, and with jeans. A tailored jacket smartens up the whole outfit.

**SCARF** A large scarf tied over the lapels of the jacket softens the sharp line of the neck and introduces a less formal element.

81

**DENIM** Clean, well-fitting jeans are casual but look smart when teamed with a jacket and a well-cut top.

**SUIT FABRIC** A trouser suit in a dark, supple fabric is a very useful item as the jacket, in particular, can be teamed with various trouser styles.

**SHOES** Stylish, highcut shoes look very attractive with formal trousers – better than boots, which would look too heavy.

**BOOTS** Boots are comfortable, hard-wearing and look good with trousers made of heavier fabrics, such as jeans or chinos.

# OLDER WOMEN

Older women, probably no longer working and definitely not lugging children about everyday, have no one to please but themselves. But this does not mean that style should disappear – their appearance is still an indication of how they wish to be viewed, and comfy cardies and granny slippers will do nothing for their own self esteem. Not a youngster myself, I counsel comfort, style and dignity. This will not necessarily be the style of earlier years – if necessary, older bones and muscles need to be considered and cared for. But, even so, this does not mean that you cannot look as good as the rest of them!

**SCARF** A loose scarf softens the neck line and introduces colour to your outfit. It can also help disguise your neck and keep it warm.

**SHOES** Loafers are extremely comfortable, put no strain on the back, look great with trousers and are easy to slip on.

**SUIT** Soft, fluid fabric is kind to your bodyshape and falls beautifully. A looser cut may be adviseable if you no longer wish to emphasize your middle.

**SHOES** Low-heeled court shoes will dress up your trousers. Square toes and a highcut tongue ensure comfort and elegance.

**TROUSERS** Loose trousers are stylish and comfortable. Comfort waistbands are now available, which means you do not have to bother with zips and buttons.

' *My two-bag system – a big one with handles for work and a smaller one for personal items – has improved my back problems no end.* '

PAMELA SMITH, FREELANCE EDITOR

Non-working women can usually get by with smaller bags and can choose from shoulder-strap styles or bags with two handles. But make sure that your bag is the right size for your requirements, since overfilling it will ruin the shape.

**Tip:** When you are buying a bag, be sure to check that the zips and clasps are of good quality and the handles are securely attached.

If you carry a straw bag or one with a rough surface, make sure that you do not wear it with clothing that will pill – I know of several people who have ruined garments this way.

WATCH

If you have one watch that you love, you'll never want to change it, so it's worth investing in a classic style that you'll have forever. The size should be in proportion with your arms, wrists and fingers. Delicate styles look very pretty on slim hands and wrists whereas bigger watches suit chunkier arms and wrists.

GLOVES

One good pair of leather gloves should last you forever. Buy them in either black or brown and, for added warmth, choose a pair that is lined. Many styles are trimmed with stitching at the top. Make sure that these are properly finished off (i.e. not left raw but with the seams finished inside the glove).

**Tip:** However tempting, scrunching up your gloves will stretch the leather and distort the shape. Store them flat.

FORMAL EVENING WEAR

Most people don't wear formal evening wear often so it need not be part of your capsule wardrobe. By accessorizing your suit, especially if it is a dark colour, you can cover several formal occasions.

**BELTS AND BUCKLES**

Buy one classic, good-quality belt in either black or brown depending on your shoe choice. But avoid flashy designer logo buckles. They date too quickly and can look overly ostentatious.

83

One good pair of leather gloves should last you forever. Buy them in either black or brown ...

# Special Occasions

*Special occasions present a wardrobe dilemma that sends the majority of women into a mild panic. Not only will every other guest be making an extra effort, but they will all be assessing each other more than usual.*

It's always at special occasions that people give one another the "once over". Whether women are attending a wedding, christening, garden party or business conference abroad, they know that they are on show, hence that all-too familiar panic, "What on earth am I going to wear?" You look at your wardrobe, full of clothes, and yet nothing seems to be exactly right.

In this chapter I aim to remove that stress. Knowledge breeds confidence so by following a few practical, simple guidelines, your next special occasion, and all those to come, should be a breeze.

### FORMAL DAYTIME EVENTS

The danger with formal daytime events, such as weddings, christenings, graduations and some lunches, particularly if you have a special rôle such as mother of the bride, is that trousers are not suitable and the outfit required can look extremely matronly.

If you're at all unsure about how to get the look right with a dress, I would advise you to buy a smart suit, either a skirt and jacket or a dress and matching jacket or coat, in a special fabric in a pretty colour, such as shantung silk, light-weight wool or velvet, depending on the season. Such a suit will take you absolutely everywhere except for Black-tie events that include dinner and dancing.

Some occasions will demand a hat. In this instance always buy your dress first and then take it with you when you buy the hat. It's a big mistake to buy the hat without wearing the dress as you will need to check that your outfit as a whole is in perfect proportion. If it is

> "What on earth am I going to wear?" You look at your wardrobe, full of clothes, and yet nothing seems to be exactly right.

**TIP**

● A dress and jacket are widely accepted at a formal daytime party and it will be less trouble for you since you don't have to think about what top to wear underneath.

● If you're wearing a dress under a jacket, buy one with either very short sleeves or no sleeves at all. It will be more comfortable than wearing one with long sleeves and it will sit neatly under the jacket.

## DRESS CODES: WHAT TO WEAR TO WHAT OCCASION

If you are going to a party or an event and are unsure of the dress code, the best way to find out is either by asking the host directly or asking someone else who will be attending the party. If both of these options prove impossible, wear an outfit that can be adapted on arrival if necessary. A smart black trouser suit with a camisole underneath is an outfit that can easily be adjusted. Keep the jacket on if the occasion proves to be less formal than you thought or take it off to reveal the camisole and add some jewellery (hidden away in your handbag) if you need to dress up.

' *I've always been interested in a woman who is busy, who travels, who is confident with her image and who doesn't buy extravagant evening-wear, but will dress up daywear for night.* '

MICHAEL KORS, FASHION DESIGNER

physically impossible for you do to this, then you should buy the hat with the shop's assurance that you can return it should it prove unsuitable.

For formal daytime events, avoid anything that is too revealing. Plunging necklines and very short skirts are a bad idea because they give off the wrong signals. You should be dressing with a certain amount of formality. If you're attending or hosting a company dinner, you don't want to give the impression of being too prim and proper but remember there is a fine line between being fashionable and flirty.

## CORPORATE EVENING ENTERTAINING

If your job does involve a great deal of work-related socializing, then choose at least one suit that is not too sharply tailored and can be worn with a dressy silk shirt or T-shirt. This should see you through cocktail parties and dinner engagements immediately after work. But to expand the ideas outlined in the capsule wardrobe (see pp. 72-83), your most useful investment would be a tailored evening jacket in a "dressy" or textured fabric. This still denotes structure and formality in your style, but looks more glamorous. It is also just the thing if you are unsure as to how dressy you should look; you can have something plain underneath if you are in fear of over-dressing and something smarter and more revealing if you think that you might be in danger of underplaying the situation.

For more formal occasions you can look glamorous, but do try to avoid anything overtly revealing that could be read as vulgar. Company dinners can be a strain for partners of employees but don't be tempted to dress "down" or play safe, whichever category you belong in. If you are a guest you should do your partner credit: there's nothing so humiliating as having an eye cast over you that implies, "… and that insignificant person is his/her partner?" Meeting someone's partner is like meeting a boyfriend's parents for the first time – you would like there to be an immediate rapport!

**Modern classics from your capsule wardrobe should equip you for more casual business activities.**

## CASUAL CORPORATE EVENTS

Modern classics from your capsule wardrobe should equip you for more casual business activities. Your jacket can be accessorized with well-cut cotton or gabardine trousers or jeans. A light-coloured linen suit will equip you for occasions such as Ascot or Wimbledon. A navy suit jacket worn with jeans and deck-shoes could provide the basic wardrobe for a sailing weekend.

When men are asked what clothes are suitable for a particular event, they are usually non-committal. But comments such as "just wear something nice" or "it's quite casual" don't really help. That's why I think it's worth investing in a casual trouser suit for these sort of functions because you can dress the suit up or down. In the summer wear a cotton suit with a pair of deck-shoes or sporty loafers and a tank top underneath the jacket. For a smarter look, replace these with some pretty sandals and a crisp shirt. For winter, buy a more relaxed, unstructured jacket with matching trousers in a textured wool. This will look stylish with both chunky knits or sophisticated shirts.

## BLACK-TIE EVENTS

Dressing for a Black-tie party is more restricting. If the event is just dinner, a dress to the knee or mid-calf, or a dark-coloured trouser suit worn with an

### TIPS

● If you don't want to wear a suit, a leather jacket is a useful (and sexy) alternative to wear with either jeans or well-cut trousers for a casual event.

● There's nothing worse than arriving at a party dressed to the nines only to discover that noone else is. I believe that of the two, it is better to be underdressed than overdressed. If I'm at all worried about being overdressed, I play it down and take some extra jewellery with me in my bag, which I wear if I feel that I need that extra pizzazz. Wearing neutral colours also helps. White and cream in the summer look both smart and casual as do black, navy or dark green in winter.

● If you want to add a shot of colour do it with your shoes, your handbag or a scarf. Evening make-up can also be colourful and sparkly.

evening top underneath, or an evening skirt suit would be suitable. But if the evening includes dinner and dancing, you can either wear a tuxedo yourself (tuxedos have remained fashionable for women since Yves Saint Laurent launched Le Smoking in the 1960s) or an evening trouser suit with a glitzy top underneath so that you can remove the jacket. Most women will feel more comfortable in a straight, ankle-length dress with perhaps a back or side split. Full, floor-sweeping dresses can look dated. Sleeveless evening dresses do look wonderful (and they keep you cool if you're dancing) but if you wish to cover your arms wear a dress with cap, short or long sleeves. Avoid wearing sleeves that end at the elbow, which can be ageing on all but the youngest of women.

Alternatively, you can wear a short dress but, if you do, it will need to be extremely fashionable or made from a truly luxurious fabric such as one that is lace or beaded. A plain, short dress looks very dull.

## COLOUR

Black is always a safe bet (don't forget, men's dinner suits are always black). Black is also the most slimming of colours which, if your shape is less than perfect, is always a good thing. However, dark jewel colours such as jade green, midnight blue, rich chocolate or wine look beautiful for evening. For summer parties you may want to try honey colours or blues too. If you can only afford one evening dress, buy it in a dark colour as you can wear it all year round. If you wish to add a little more colour, do so with your jewellery, makeup or with a shawl or wrap that you can wear if you feel cold.

87

### GLASSES

Glasses are just as important as jewellery or any other accessory. If you wear glasses every day, it's definitely worth investing in a pair to wear for smart occasions because some frames, such as tortoiseshell, for example, will look very heavy with a fine silk evening gown. Choose your evening glasses to match your jewellery: if most of your jewellery is gold, wear "gold" frames, if it's silver then choose "silver" frames.

## FABRICS

Black jersey is my fabric of choice for evening. It hangs wonderfully, is easy to look after and it never dates. Winter fabrics such as velvet often look luxurious, but you can feel too hot in them, particularly if you are dancing. If you have a tendency to feel the heat, make sure that the style of dress that you choose allows for some skin exposure – either bare arms or a good décolleté.

## JEWELLERY

Jewellery should be kept to a minimum. Some women use formal occasions to put on everything that they possess, simply to show us that they've got it. Personally, I think piling on the jewellery in this way is very ugly. As with your daytime outfits, put on your dress and then see what jewellery, if any, it requires. As a general rule, the glitzier the dress, the less jewellery you should wear.

   **Tip:** If you have jewellery that you want to wear, take it (or a picture) with you when buying your evening dress to make sure that it suits the styles and colours of the dresses that you are considering.

## SHOES AND BAGS

For all special occasions, you need to be aware that, like your jewellery, your shoes and your handbag are very important. Unless they are gold or silver, they don't necessarily need to match, but if you decide to wear a colour such as red or green, either your bag or your shoes should be the same colour as your outfit. Your evening bag should not detract from what you are wearing, so keep your belongings to an absolute minimum and carry a small bag, which fits snugly under your arm. I find a clutch most useful because they have a handle you can put over your wrist if necessary – it's awful when you're carrying a bag in one hand, a drink in the other and then being offered a canapé that you have to refuse! Remember that when you're wearing fine fabric and soft styles of clothing in the evening, the proportions of your bag should also be feminine so that it won't detract from your outfit.

## HATS

Hats can look wonderful but remember that they can be a real burden for the person sitting behind you, particularly at a wedding.

Tip: When wearing a hat it's a good idea to carry a hand-mirror as what a hat looks like from the front bears no relation to what it looks like at the back.

### UNDERWEAR

Wearing tights with an in-built gusset means that you won't need to wear briefs. This will create a much smoother line, which is particularly important for dresses that are made from fine fabrics such as silk and satin. (For further information see Lingerie pp. 62–65.)

### WHAT TO PUT ON TOP

Women often tell me that they never know what to put on top of their evening dresses for Black-tie events because their everyday coats look wrong.

In the old days it was common practice for women to wear fur over their evening wear. Today of course, most women don't, either because they don't want to, or because they don't dare to. If you like fur, there are plenty of faux fur jackets available. But nowadays, a large stole or pashmina in a pretty colour is most useful. Personally, I prefer to wear a coat or jacket in an unusual fabric over a long evening dress. Otherwise, if I want a modern, casual look, I wear a fitted, leather jacket.

89

### CHANGING IN THE OFFICE

If you are going to a formal dinner party during the week after work and don't have time to go home first, make sure that you leave enough time the night before to get yourself ready. Wear a dressy suit to the office, a little fitted jacket, for example, which can be worn without a top underneath, with a straight skirt, and take a pair of evening sandals, an evening bag, jewellery and a spare

**It's always useful to have a second set of make-up and brushes in your desk at work...**

pair of tights. When you are ready to go out, remove the top you've been wearing under your jacket, change your earrings, add a piece of jewellery if you wish, swap your day shoes for your evening shoes or sandals, change your handbag and redo your make-up. It's always useful to have a second set of make-up and brushes in your desk at work, otherwise you will need to bring your make-up with you.

Alternatives could include a dress and matching jacket, swapping a daytime chiffon scarf for evening jewellery, or a black trouser suit, which you could dress up in the evening by exchanging your blouse for a dressy top, such as one that is beaded or with a bit of glitter.

**Tip:** Try to do your make-up in natural light by a window as the fluorescent light often found in cloakrooms can flatten your features and may encourage you to apply too much make-up.

GOING TO A PREMIERE

If you are going straight from the office to a première or other, very formal evening event which requires something much dressier, you will have to bring your dress to the office in a hanging bag. Hang the dress up so that the creases can drop out during the course of the day. You will also need to bring your evening shoes, jewellery and shawl or evening coat. Make sure that the underwear you put on in the morning is the right cut for your evening dress.
If you are wearing a strapless dress, it's a good idea to either wear a strapless bra or to loosen your bra straps several hours before getting changed to allow time for the strap marks to disappear.

## OTHER CONSIDERATIONS

For some people there are other considerations that need to be made when deciding what to wear to a formal function. Wheelchair users, for example, have often said to me that they are at a loss as to what to wear to functions where they want to look glamorous.

In this situation, I would suggest that you concentrate on making your top half look as good as possible as this is the part that people will notice the most. I would suggest you wear a really smart jacket and a pretty scarf or shawl, which will add an elegant touch of colour to your outfit while keeping you warm too. For a younger look, try a simple black dress with a scoop neckline and wear a wonderful cardigan loosely knotted around your neck. Your feet will also be more visible, so a pair of shoes that you like will also give you confidence. Feeling good is the key to enjoying any special occasion so making that extra effort, perhaps a visit to the hairdresser, is well worth it.

Check your shoes for scuff marks and other damage.

90

> ' *There is one certain thing about a well-dressed woman, she has taken trouble. And to take trouble is to strengthen character.* '
>
> ROBERT LYND, JOURNALIST AND ESSAYIST

## PAMPER YOURSELF

It's worth pampering yourself for an important occasion. If you are going to be wearing sandals that expose your toes, have a pedicure. Similarly, it's worth having an exfoliating and moisturizing back treatment if you're going to wear a backless dress. Always make sure that you leave enough time to prepare yourself without having to rush.

### THE SPECIAL OCCASION CHECKLIST

Your routine, and not just for a special occasion, should begin two weeks beforehand and include the following:

- Book a manicure, pedicure and exfoliating treatment.

- Check to see whether your clothes are clean. Do they need altering? Are the buttons and zips secure?

- Do you have the right tights? Always pack a spare pair in your evening bag. They take up very little space and can save you much embarrassment should you discover a ladder in your tights as you're about to hit the dance floor!

- Check your shoes for scuff marks and other damage. Clean them.

- Book an appointment at the hairdresser.

- Does your jewellery need to be cleaned?

- Pack your handbag and, if necessary, your overnight case, in advance so that you don't forget anything at the last minute.

- If you need a cab, book one the day before or earlier in the day and ring later to check that your booking has not been lost.

- Even if you don't expect to need any money, always take enough for a taxi fare home – in case of emergency. Two or three 10p pieces are also useful in case you need to use a payphone.

- The night before, get a good night's sleep – the greater your energy, the greater your confidence will be.

It's worth having an exfoliating and moisturizing back treatment if you're going to wear a backless dress.

# Dresses

*Ten years ago, when I wrote my first book, the choice of dresses, with the exception of long summer dresses made from linen or poplin or perhaps a coat dress for work, was limited and somewhat frumpy.*

## CHOOSING THE RIGHT JACKET FOR YOUR DRESS

If you already own the jacket, take it when you shop for your dress. Slip the jacket over the dress and treat the dress as two separate pieces. Does the neckline of your "top" sit well under the jacket? Similarly, does the "skirt" suit the shape of the jacket.? Does it need to be tapered? Is the length in proportion with that of the jacket? Do the fabrics complement one another? Remember, the jacket should always be made from a heavier fabric than the dress. I always recommend the shift dress, with or without a sleeve, since, due to the simplicity of its cut, it suits most jacket shapes.

However, because the jacket has now become such an integral part of everyday dressing, women are looking for something other than a skirt or a pair of trousers to wear with it and more choice has emerged. On top of that, dresses are incredibly easy to adapt from day to evening wear. All you need to do is change your shoes, put your essentials in a smaller bag, perhaps add a beaded scarf or cardigan, a touch of lipstick *et voilà*! You're ready in seconds.

## DRESS STYLES

The most recent dress to emerge is the basic shift dress, which is usually fitted and is produced in various fabrics, lengths and with different sleeves.

If the top of your arms pass muster, a sleeveless shift dress is ideal, even in winter, as it fits neatly under a jacket. Otherwise, try a small cap sleeve or a short sleeve. Choose the length of your sleeve in relation to the condition of your arms and elbows (rather like you should choose skirt lengths depending on the quality of your knees).

Although I prefer sleeveless dresses, long-sleeved dresses can look incredibly elegant. But finding a jacket to wear with it is no mean feat. I would save it for occasions when a jacket isn't called for and put an interesting coat over it instead.

The shirt-dress and the wrap-dress are two styles of day dresses that regularly come in and out of fashion. But, like the long-sleeved dress, finding a suitable jacket to wear over the top can be quite tricky. However, during the warm summer months when no jacket is required, they are both stylish and easy to wear.

## FABRIC AND COLOUR

Dress cloth needs to be fluid because it should move with the body. Thick, bulky materials are unlikely to lie well and are impractical if you work in a warm office. Pure wool (with or without Lycra) is the most useful fabric as it is fine and light enough to wear in the summer too. In terms of colour, apply the same considerations (neutral monochromes) as you would to a skirt or a pair of trousers, as your dress needs to complement the rest of your wardrobe.

## ACCESSORIES

Wear accessories, because otherwise your dress is one unbroken line or chunk of fabric, with nothing to pull the eye upwards. This often results in your legs becoming the focus of attention.

## SHOES

One of the reasons why I love the shift dress is because it suits virtually every style of shoe from traditional court shoe styles to sexier kitten heels. Flat shoes do very little for a woman's legs unless the wearer's calves are unusually long and slim. Heels ranging from 2–6cm (1–2 $\frac{1}{2}$in) are generally more flattering.

## EVENING DRESSES

Gone are the days when prom or frothy "meringue" dresses were fashionable – thank goodness! When shopping for an evening dress, always follow the principle "Less is More". Also, remember that eveningwear dates far less than daywear so you will need less and you'll probably meet different people each time you're wearing it. Wear long or short sleeves but if you do wear short, again, pay attention to your elbows. Like the neck and hands, elbows are an indication of age.

**When shopping for an evening dress, always follow the principle "Less is More".**

Be careful of bias-cut dresses. Cut on the diagonal – rather than straight up and down – they accentuate every curve. This makes them difficult to wear and they look best on slim, well-proportioned figures. They must also be beautifully made to look good.

# Makeover *Ayesha*

**A**yesha is a recent graduate, and would like to break into the world of media or advertising. She wants a look that will help her project a confident, credible, yet relaxed image.

## BEFORE

Ayesha's style had not had time to develop since her university days, so she still looked very much like a student. The length of her hair, coupled with the long, loose dress pulled the eye away from her face and gave the impression that she didn't feel at ease with herself or give much thought to her appearance. The length of the dress also contributed to making Ayesha look bigger than her slim size 10.

## WHAT WE DECIDED TO DO

We wanted to counteract a seeming insecurity, project Ayesha's vibrancy and youth and give her the confidence to meet and impress employers. We opted for shoulder-length hair, which is stylish but still young and pretty, and set out to find her flattering work clothes that would look appropriate for the job she was hoping to get.

## CLOTHES

As a graduate Ayesha is on a budget and wanted clothes that would give her maximum use, so versatility was a key requirement. Media and advertising are fairly relaxed and social environments, which meant it was easy to suggest clothes that she could wear from day to evening. We decided on a textured wool twinset that could be worn either together or separately. Short and small-framed women must be careful that they are not overwhelmed by knitwear (turn to p. 96)

## As a graduate she is on a budget

94

> *' I like my shorter haircut. It really felt as if a weight was off my shoulders and I immediately felt very relaxed and jolly. '*
> AYESHA

**TWIN SET** A textured, short-sleeved sweater gives both comfort and a youthful look. Worn with a matching cardigan, it is, in a less formal working environment, a great alternative to a jacket and blouse. The two pieces have the additional advantage of working as separates within a capsule wardrobe.

**POLO NECK** This small, rolled neck adds detail without clutter. It works perfectly with Ayesha's new shorter hairstyle.

**JEWELLERY** Very simple and youthful jewellery finishes off the outfit. A pair of stud earrings, a watch and a ring complement the uncluttered simplicity of Ayesha's look.

**95**

**SCARF** As a cooler alternative to the twin set, Ayesha could team a shirt and unconstructed jacket with a large scarf or pashmina gently knotted around her neck.

**SHOES** This high-cut, lace-up shoe with a mid-height heel lends Ayesha extra height. By hiding all of the foot, it also elongates the leg by giving the impression of a continuous, unbroken line. The modern, grey flannel fabric suits the shoes, which are a comfortable and creative accessory.

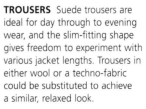

**TROUSERS** Suede trousers are ideal for day through to evening wear, and the slim-fitting shape gives freedom to experiment with various jacket lengths. Trousers in either wool or a techno-fabric could be substituted to achieve a similar, relaxed look.

that is often too bulky for their size. Although Ayesha is petite, the weight of the twinset complements her figure rather than camouflaging it. Falling just below the waist, the sweater will inspire confidence for anyone self-conscious about their stomach and, as it is not too bulky, it can be worn under jackets with either trousers or skirts. The zip-up cardigan is warm enough to wear as a relaxed substitute for a jacket and could be worn with a plain cotton T-shirt underneath.

**"techno" fabrics are a budget-friendly substitute for suede**

Suede trousers are comfortable, trendy and suitable for formal and informal occasions. Contrary to popular myth, suede is suitable for both summer and winter. Although it is quite hard-wearing, it must be cleaned by a specialist. Otherwise, modern "techno" fabrics are a budget-friendly substitute for suede and easier to clean.

Ayesha's outfit called for quite a chunky shoe – anything too light would have been incongruous with the fabrics that we chose. To avoid making the look too masculine, however, we chose lace-up shoes with a pretty heel. These are a classic style, can be worn with other items and gave Ayesha a little more height.

Ayesha's new look has given her a lively and vibrant image, which is fashionable, creative and relaxed. It is simple and youthful – ideal for securing that all-important first job.

*'Your eyebrow should line up with the inside corner of your eye; it should arch three-quarters of the way along, and extend to the far end where it should taper down very slightly.'*

MAGGIE HUNT, MAKE-UP ARTIST

## HAIR

Ayesha's hair was very long, and had no definite style. The length obscured her face and gave her the impression of having very rounded shoulders. We cut it to shoulder-length and blunted the ends to add volume. We also layered the hair around the face to add body and movement, which had the effect of softening her features. The cut encouraged a natural curl that was very attractive.

## MAKE-UP

It used to be difficult for women with African or Asian complexions to find make-up – especially foundation – that suited their skin. Now there are brands, such as Fashion Fair, Iman, Mac and Bobbi Brown, designed for darker or yellow-based skins.

We matched a foundation to Ayesha's natural skin tone and then used black khol around her eyes. We kept her lips soft and understated to give a natural look that wouldn't age her. Ayesha's eyebrows were the feature most in need of attention. They were bushy and uneven and their shape made her face look a little sad. To improve their balance they needed to be plucked and reshaped.

### ASIAN AND AFRICAN SKINS

Asian and African skins are more yellow-toned than northern European skins. But whatever the colour of your skin, the most important thing is to match your foundation or concealer precisely to your skin colour. If you use powder, this too should match. Try to use brands that specialize in make-up for dark skins as these will be more effective. On the whole, avoid colours that have too much red in them, although slightly pink tones may suit some African skins. Avoid using anything that claims to lighten your skin. These usually give an artificial pallor and rob the skin of its natural warmth. Blusher in tones of warm peach, light brown or cinnamon with a light, translucent texture suits black skins; plum and dusky pinks lift Asian skins. Dark lipstick, which looks vampy on pale skins, can be wonderful on darker skins. Strong pinks do not tone well with black skin. Avoid pale pinks if you have skin that has a very yellow tone as these can look draining. Deeper shades of pink or plum look better.

### EYEBROW SHAPING

A well-shaped brow can improve the shape of the eye, particularly helping women with small, deep-set eyes, and often makes eye make-up less necessary. Be careful when plucking your eyebrows. Never pluck them too heavily, too far apart or from above. Nor should you cut them as this will make them grow even longer and thicker. If your eyebrows are excessively long then you will have to trim them. But once you start, you can never stop. Comb them up and trim one by one.

# Evaluating Your Wardrobe

*Changes in your life, such as a new job, getting married or divorced, may mean that you feel the need to reorganize or revitalize your wardrobe in order to present yourself in a new way for a new era.*

Now is the time to take a careful and truthful look at your wardrobe, whether you are more in the public eye than before, entering a new decade (see p.10), a new mode of life, or moving house and rationalizing all your possessions.

Gaining or losing a lot of weight will mean that some clothes no longer fit properly and, like many women, you may possess clothing that ranges over several sizes, catering for fluctuations in your weight. Take this opportunity to discard that fantasy of ever being a size 10 again and resolve to make the very best of your larger frame through skilled shopping. Reorganize your wardrobe as part of a new resolution to be more organized generally.

If you have spent years buying clothes without scheme, analysis or detailed planning, then examining your wardrobe can be very chastening! You are likely to find that you have lots of clothes that don't work together terribly well. Impulse buys, fashion fads or clothes in shades that don't blend with the rest of your wardrobe may need to be discarded. Don't feel guilty, feel confident – your life will be far more hassle-free by having a well-managed wardrobe.

> *' Good items never die. '*
> RALPH LAUREN,
> FASHION DESIGNER

**TIP**

Take this opportunity to thoroughly clean out your wardrobe. Hoover, wipe down shelves and get some lavender bags or cedar wood - these are the most efficient anti-moth devices.

## QUALITY NOT QUANTITY

It is important to say here that owning a large number of clothes has little bearing on whether you present yourself well or not, and that a woman who dresses with style does not need to wear something different to work every day of the week. Obviously, you want choice and versatility from your clothes but this has as much to do with their quality, in the broadest sense of the word, as from their quantity. Even more important is their flexibility to be worn in different ways by changing accessories.

Owning a large number of clothes has little bearing on whether you present yourself well or not and... a woman who dresses with style does not need to wear something different to work every day...

98

## WEEDING OUT

Now that you have decided to cut back to the necessary items, pick out the clothes you like and wear a lot. Analyse why you like them. Have people told you that the colour suits you? Does the fit feel good, the cut flatter your figure? Is the cloth easy to clean and crease resistant? Some favourite clothes will defy analysis and simply be garments to which you feel emotionally attached. If they are redolent of affectionate memories, hang on to them as you would any other souvenir – they are, after all, a part of your history.

While sifting through these "old favourites", try them on and check their condition – make a note if they need cleaning or repairs. They're all part of your appearance and the "messages" you send to people around you. Check too, that skirt linings haven't worn out or trousers lost their shape by bagging at the bottom or knees. If they have, accept that they are past redemption.

Now look at the clothes that you no longer wear, or were obvious mistakes. If you haven't worn an item for two years of more, you should probably remove it. Anything that does not fit properly and cannot be altered, that has an exaggerated, out-of-date cut should be discarded. It will be hard, but it's got to be done!

I'd also advise you to include lingerie and jewellery in this overhaul. It's easy to hoard jewellery because it takes up so little space. This can make it difficult to choose the right pieces quickly for the outfit that you are wearing.

As for lingerie and hosiery, you will know when it's past its "sell-by date" – just get rid of it. If you organize your tights by denier and colour, you will find your life easier.

Most of us have a weakness for some sort of accessory: some women are "bagaholics", others love shoes and some own dozens of belts. Now is the time to acknowledge this fetish and rationalize it! Work out just how often you've worn an accessory and whether this warrants the space it is taking up in your wardrobe.

## SAVING CLOTHES FOR "NEXT TIME"

As fashion is cyclical, you may be tempted to keep things "for next time". But, rest assured, the next time something comes around, it will have been modified in some way or technological

### HOW TO EDIT YOUR WARDROBE

● Leave the items you are certain you want to keep in your wardrobe. Take everything else out and put it into a big pile on the floor.

● Try on every garment from the pile and ask yourself, "does it still look good on me?" Is the shape dated? If I saw it in a shop now, would I still want to buy it?

● Now, split this pile into three smaller ones as follows:
a) Items you'd like to hang on to.
b) Items you've worn during the past two years but not very often.
c) Items you haven't worn at all during the past two years.

● Put pile a) back in your wardrobe.

● Reassess pile b) and be ruthless.

● Put what is left of pile b) back in the wardrobe (this will probably become next time's pile c).

● Take pile c) to a charity shop, a second-hand boutique or give them to someone who can make use of them.

This principle should be applied to everything except for eveningwear and coats as these last many years without dating as quickly as the rest of your wardrobe.

developments in fabric manufacture, cutting, cloth, and dyeing will have become more sophisticated. So, you may think that jackets from the 1980s and the 1940s look very similar, but technological development will mean that they are, in fact, quite different.

You might wish to sell the clothes that you no longer want, or give them to a deserving cause. If you find that many of your clothes are redundant, don't be disheartened. Analyse what was wrong with the cut, cloth and colour; resolve not to make those errors again and to buy high-fashion garments with more discretion!

## MAKING LISTS

Once you have sifted through your clothes, draw up a list of everything that remains in your wardrobe. When you go shopping for new clothes, take this with you (either physically or mentally) and you will find that it helps enormously. So will taking a polaroid of the clothes you're trying to match up. To remind yourself of the proportions and fit, take a polaroid of yourself wearing the garment. Your description of each item should follow the basic "cut, colour, cloth" guidelines – for example, "one straight skirt with front split, black wool". This is so that you get the proportion of your purchases correct, with the cut and the thickness of the cloth chosen to complement the garment you are trying to match (see pp. 76-87).

Give yourself plenty of time to do your reappraisal. If you rush, then you might discard clothes impulsively, and regret it later. Take the time to consider what suits you and why it feels comfortable.

## BUT WILL I HAVE ANYTHING LEFT?

Many women delay editing their wardrobes for fear that there will be nothing left in it! However, if you're not wearing most of the clothes that you possess, then they might as well not exist. Remember, having a few, better-quality, classic clothes and accessories is preferable to having a wardrobe full of clothes that you never wear. If you suddenly have lots of space in your wardrobe, be excited about gradually filling it up as and when you can afford it with clothes that you will actually wear.

**Many women delay editing their wardrobes for fear that there will be nothing left in it!**

### WHAT TO KEEP

Although I'm all for a concise wardrobe, there are some items that are worth keeping – for example, classic white shirts and neutrally-coloured cashmere sweaters. There are some items I will never get rid. My 10-year-old, long, white, slim-fitting cashmere coat, for example, can be worn as an evening coat in the winter or over a trouser suit in the spring; it will never date and, although it was extremely expensive, I've certainly got my money's worth. Good clothes will always stand the test of time. But don't think that clothes are only worth keeping if they are very expensive. There's no need to discard one of your favourite sweaters just because it's not up-to-the-minute. If you love it, keep it for lounging around in. Similarly, sporty clothes such as jeans and sweatshirts never go out of fashion, so keep them as well.

' *I used to have far too many clothes although I complained that I had nothing to wear! A large amount of time and money was spent on clothes* '

CHARLOTTE WEBB, CORPORATE COMMUNICATIONS MANAGER

## BUILDING ON WHAT'S LEFT

Even if you have been buying clothes in the most whimsical, arbitrary way, some colours will predominate. Take the most predominant neutral as the base colour in your new wardrobe. This is not as restricting as it sounds, as groups of neutrals are highly compatible – taupes, creams, tans, camels and browns can mix very well with blacks and greys.

Using neutrals as the basis for your wardrobe need not mean that you will end up looking dull and colourless (see pp. 78–87). If you choose navy as a predominant neutral, you could also choose pale grey, which is a complete contrast. The two look good together and, when worn separately, look smart with splashes of powder-blue, for example. Consider your colouring when choosing neutrals. For instance, if you have a yellow-based complexion, cold colours such as black and grey will look less good than warmer creams, ivories or browns.

Using neutrals as the basis for your wardrobe need not mean that you will end up looking dull...

You may find that although you have enough tailored clothes, the rest looks jaded and dull. If you are not getting enough wear out of a jacket or skirt, you may not have the right blouse for it. As a change from tailored lines, a cotton or wool knitted two-piece is comfortable and smart enough for work. But remember, you still need to pair it with a jacket in your wardrobe.

If you are developing a new wardrobe, don't choose a radically different style from your old one without professional guidance – unless you are absolutely sure that it is a style with which you are comfortable. Planning your wardrobe from the basis of a jacket or a suit, you should only need to make one or two major purchases per season.

Now that you have read this section, I hope that you now understand why less is definitely more!

101

# Accessories

❖

*The right accessories can make an outfit look like a million dollars, the wrong accessories will make a million dollar outfit look ordinary.*

# Jewellery

*There is no doubt that jewellery can dramatically change the look of your entire outfit but, more important, it is the key to expressing your individuality.*

This chapter will show you how to incorporate jewellery and other accessories into your capsule wardrobe, and how to wear them with confidence and style.

### JEWELLERY

More than any other fashion accessory, jewellery comes and goes in cycles. In the 1970s, ethnic jewellery was all the rage; in the 1980s, gold worn in large chunks (and lots of it!) was used as a status symbol and sign of wealth. Since then, small, discreet jewellery has become far more fashionable. We are living in a society today that doesn't necessarily wish to show its wealth; style has taken precedence. When you look at people's watches now (unlike in the 1980s when the Rolex had its heyday), it is difficult to know whether they are worth £100 or £1,000. Similarly, it is difficult to know whether a pair of earrings is made from silver, white gold or platinum. The current trend for discreet jewellery is largely due to the fact that the clothes being worn now are minimalist and fitted. Shoulders are narrower and jewellery, as with all other accessories, must be in proportion to the clothes that you wear. Whereas the wide shoulder-padded jackets of the 1980s were perfect for balancing out large earrings, the same earrings worn with a deconstructed jacket would look top heavy.

**Jewellery, as with all other accessories, must be in proportion to the clothes that you wear.**

### GOLD OR SILVER?

Choosing to wear either gold or silver jewellery is rather like deciding what colour your clothes should be. Try it on and see what suits you. As a general rule, those with pale skin (i.e. a classic English Rose complexion) look better in silver, as do those with silver-grey hair.

Silver jewellery also complements clothes worn in shades of grey, blue, stark white and black.

Gold jewellery looks better on those with yellow-based skins and with honey, ivory, brown and beige clothing. I, personally, prefer gold as it is warm and throws soft light on to the skin. But should you dislike both gold and silver, pearls, particularly pearl earrings, are a useful accessory. They suit every complexion, can be worn with all clothing, regardless of colour, and, like gold, they cast a flattering light onto the face. When you are deciding what to wear, it is generally better not to mix gold and silver, although there are no hard and fast rules. I generally pick either a gold or silver watch and work my jewellery around it.

## SUITABLE JEWELLERY

Jewellery should never look obtrusive with business dress and if your clothes are chic, large amounts of jewellery will detract from them. Steer clear of heavy, attention-grabbing pieces, which make you look like a Christmas tree, and wear small, discreet shapes in gold, silver or pearl instead. If you need to attend a social function straight after work, swapping your everyday earrings for some dressier ones, or adding a necklace is a quick, practical way of transforming a day look into an evening one.

**If your clothes are chic, large amounts of jewellery will detract from them.**

## RECYCLE YOUR JEWELLERY

Since trends move fast in the jewellery world it is always worth hanging on to what you have – you never know when a trend will come back into fashion. However, there are times when it is worth redesigning jewellery. A number of years ago I was left a diamond ring by an aunt, but I didn't like the design. Rather than leave it in the vault of a bank untouched and unworn, I had the stone reset in a modern design. In fact, I've had it redesigned a number of times. To me, what is important is the sentimental value that the diamond holds. Whenever I wear it, I think of my aunt and know that she would be happy to know that I enjoy wearing it regularly.

# Shoes & Boots

*Most of us have far too large a collection of disparate footwear. Cut, cloth, colour – although in a slightly different sense – have relevance again here, as does my "less is more" theory.*

By thinking first and buying later, you can accessorize sensibly with shoes and complement your working wardrobe perfectly, as well as economically.

If you buy good-quality shoes and care for them properly you should only need two pairs per season. (For shoes in your capsule wardrobe see p. 77.)

When you buy shoes, always walk around the shop in them, and make sure that they are wide enough. If you've got wide feet, it's often a good idea to go up a size and put in an inner sole. Otherwise, the width of the shoe will stretch and the toes will curl. Also, remember to allow for the fact that your feet can swell in hot weather.

Those with narrow feet should look for labels (often Italian) that specialize in narrow fittings. Shoes that are too wide or too long will constantly slip off, making you feel, and look, unsure of yourself and unsteady on your feet. If your shoes are uncomfortable it will immediately show on your face.

**When you buy shoes, always walk around the shop in them, and make sure that they are wide enough.**

### FLAT SHOES
There are two basic styles of flat shoe. The first is a moccasin or loafer, which has a $^{1}/_{2}$ cm ($^{1}/_{5}$ in) heel. The second has a $1^{1}/_{2}$ – 2cm ($^{1}/_{2}$–1in) heel. Many women (particularly those who are on the small side) feel more comfortable in the latter. They give a little height but still look flat – perfect for wearing with trousers and longer skirts.

### COURT SHOES
Of all the shoe designs on the market, the court shoe is, without doubt, the bestseller. With a heel of 3–4cm ($1$–$1^{1}/_{2}$ in), the court shoe is comfortable

to walk in and it complements most dress, skirt and trouser styles. The shape of the toes vary from season to season depending on the fashion, from rounded to square, to very pointed.

Tip: Court shoes worn with trousers look most stylish when most of the foot is covered, so buy styles where the front of the shoe is high cut if you plan to wear them with trousers.

## HEELS

Many women use 5-6cm (2–2½ in) heel height for daywear. It is slightly higher than the classic court shoe but can still be worn for everyday wear, particularly if you're in a job that allows you to drive to work and change when you get there. If not, travel in some loafers and carry your heels in your bag.

## T-STRAPS AND ANKLE STRAPS

Unless your feet, ankles and calves are some of your best features, avoid T-straps and ankle straps. They draw attention to the feet and make legs look shorter by creating lines across them. There are, however, certain ankle straps that, because of the way they are fitted to the shoe, start at a different angle and are not quite so unflattering. So, if you really fall in love with a pair, try them on just in case.

## SLING-BACKS

Again, these shoes need good ankles and calves to look flattering. They also tend to reveal heels that are in bad condition (cracked and broken skin on heels just isn't attractive). Sling-backs look best when they look modern i.e. with an open or pointed toe and a sexy kitten heel.

Court shoes worn with trousers look most stylish when most of the foot is covered, so buy styles where the front of the shoe is high cut...

107

**COURT SHOES**
The appeal of the court shoe is such that they are designed in all sorts of shapes and colours to suit different requirements. Details may change with the seasons – pointed, square or rounded toes, a higher or lower heel – but the basic idea remains the same.

**HEELS, TOES AND BACKS**
The style of heels, toes and the backs of shoes changes virtually every season. Long toes slim your feet and ankles as does a heel, although if it is too high it might make your calves look heavy. Strappy shoes should be viewed with caution as they can make your ankles look wide.

## KITTEN HEELS

Kitten heels regularly come in and go out of fashion. They are a fashion statement and are, therefore, best worn with very fashionable garments. Classic clothes don't really work with this style of shoe. However, worn correctly they can look extremely stylish with dresses, Capri pants, wide trousers and dressy suits.

## WEDGE SANDALS

Wedge sandal are a blessing for many women who don't have great legs, because contrasted against the chunky heel, chunky legs look slim. Wear wedge sandals and fake tan in the summer and you will be delighted at how your legs look.

A word of warning: try to find a style with straps as ankles are vulnerable and can easily twist.

**Tip:** Never drive in a pair of wedge sandals because it is impossible to feel the pedals through the heel. Instead keep a pair of moccasins in the car and drive in those.

## BROWN SANDALS

I always advise women to have a pair of brown leather sandals for summer. They will complement most clothes in your capsule wardrobe and they are much more versatile and practical than white or cream sandals. Those with a 3-cm (1½- in) heel are probably the most useful but this can vary depending on the shape of your legs and what you feel most comfortable wearing.

## HEEL HEIGHT

Every season, the height and shape of heels change according to the length and shape of skirts. It is all a question of proportion: if you're wearing a heavy tweed suit and you put a stiletto heel with it, proportionally it will look very unbalanced. This is why the heels of shoes tend to be heavier (and sometimes even with a platform sole) when heavier fabrics are fashionable. Conversely, delicate shoes become popular when light and airy fabrics become fashionable.

**Tip:** Whatever the fashion, always choose a heel height that feels comfortable. There is nothing worse than seeing a woman wobble. An elegant outfit will be ruined by bad posture.

## COLOUR

If you can only buy one pair of shoes, buy them in black. Neutral tones are most useful for a working wardrobe but if you love coloured shoes, buy cheaper ones in summer that you can have fun with and then throw away.

## FABRIC

Although suede and fabric shoes can be useful, they lose colour and look old quite quickly (see p. 150 for suede maintenance). Good quality leather lasts longer when properly looked after. Remember the thickness of leather will vary from summer to winter.

## A WORD ON TRAINERS

Trainers have become an essential part of every woman's wardrobe and are widely used in and out of the gym. However, if worn too often they do encourage toes to spread and, therefore, feet to widen. Youngsters especially, should be wary of wearing them too often.

**Tip:** Try to alternate your shoes (and heel height) daily. This is vital for keeping both your feet and your shoes in top condition.

## BOOTS

Ankle boots look great with trousers but little else, apart from long skirts when, depending on the fashion, they can look very chic.

I also think that knee-length boots, unless you are very young, should be worn with skirts that fall below the top edge of the boot.

**Tip:** If you have big calves and have difficulty in finding boots that fit, buy styles made from elasticated fabric or designs fitted with elasticated panels.

## SHOES FOR CHUNKY LEGS

If your legs are less than perfect, go for simple styles and avoid both very high-cut and low-cut shoes. Use a mirror when you try on shoes and look at them from all angles. Choose the style that flatters your leg. Remember, the longer the shoe the slimmer your feet and ankles will look. In summer, try a platform sandal – the added height will slim your calves.

**109**

### LOW-HEELED SHOES

Shoes with low heels are very comfortable. They are usually high-cut, so they look very good with trousers. Tall women with thin legs may wear them with skirts, although a slight heel is more elegant. Short women or women with chunky legs should only wear them with trousers or long skirts.

# Makeover *Natasha*

Natasha works in advertising in an office that is fairly casual. However, there are now times when she needs to meet clients and, on occasion, go to client dinners. She felt she needed something that gave her more gravitas and worked both in the office and for meetings or dinner after work.

### BEFORE

Before her makeover, Natasha was wearing casual clothing that belied her age and authority within the office. While this did not prove a problem within the hierarchy at work, she found that in client meetings, she was automatically assumed to be younger and more junior than she was, and that clients tended to take her less seriously than male members of staff. In terms of style, her long hair, long cardigan and long necklace also emphasized her long face and drew the eye downwards, making her look very thin.

### WHAT WE DECIDED TO DO

As Natasha was working predominantly with men – particularly in terms of the client base – she should be dressed in a suit that was feminine and sophisticated but also gave the message that she was a serious business woman. However, we didn't want to make her feel uncomfortable or deny her femininity so we had to find a way of combining our two aims. It was necessary to cut her hair, which was too long. It emphasized the length and thinness of her face and we also thought that a shorter, smarter haircut would contribute to a sharper, more chic image. It was also more in keeping with her age, especially as she was beginning to develop fine lines. I realize that if (turn to p. 112)

**Natasha wanted to be smart yet feminine in a male-dominated environment.**

**VITAL STATISTICS**

Natasha Wingate
**Age:** 37
**Height:** 5ft 5in
**Dress size:** 10
**Occupation:** Advertising
**Aim:** To project a feminine yet capable and confident appearance with clothes that could take her from the office to social events.

' *I instantly felt more confident, and very feminine at the same time.* '
NATASHA

110

**COLLAR**
The high revere means that the jacket can be worn without a top underneath, making the collar a fashion detail in itself.

**SHOULDER LINE**
A structured but not too severe shoulder line adds authority to the look and works well with soft, shoulder-length hair.

**JACKET** This beautifully fitted, four-button jacket accentuates a small waist and slim figure. The longer length gives an elegant and unbroken line which is extremely flattering.

**SKIRT** A simple, classic knee-length skirt shows off good legs and creates a sharp, modern silhouette.

111

**T-SHIRT** A light woollen or cotton T-shirt lies flat underneath the high collar. It allows the jacket to be removed for less formal occasions.

**FABRIC** The understated, pin-striped wool fabric made into a sexy-shaped suit was, we felt, a little tongue-in-cheek-humour for a woman working in a male environment. It is also practical and does not crease easily.

you have always had long hair, it's a hard decision to cut it, but I do think that women generally look better with shorter hair as they get older. Long hair, worn down, is a young style and if your skin is showing signs of ageing, a very long style will begin to look incongruous. Had Natasha wished to keep her hair long, I would have suggested that she tie it back – but be warned, if you want it to look smart, you must have attractive hair accessories.

## Women generally look better with shorter hair as they get older.

### CLOTHES

We dressed Natasha in a pinstripe suit with a cut that was feminine enough for her to feel comfortable. We chose a jacket that, when fastened, didn't need to be worn with a top underneath. Worn this way it created a "dress" effect. For a more relaxed look, it could be worn with a fine knit or short-sleeved sweater or T-shirt underneath. Jewellery would dress it up for the evening.

Since Natasha has good legs we chose a skirt length that just skimmed the knee in order to highlight her shapely calves. Mesh tights were used to avoid an over-hard image, and we completed the look with a pair of simple, stylish court shoes with a heel height appropriate to everyday use.

**112**

> *Don't worry about fine lines around the eyes. They are a sign of much laughter but can be camouflaged!*
> MAGGIE HUNT, MAKE-UP ARTIST

## MAKE-UP

Natasha's features were good and strong so we applied make-up to enhance and balance them. She had developed a few wrinkles and blemishes so we needed to apply a foundation that looked natural but gave good coverage without being obvious. We took care not to overapply because foundation will gather in lines and pores, and will emphasize wrinkles. We dusted fine powder over her foundation to set it and prevent it from melting. We used a variety of neutral, brownish shades of eyeshadow, and a warm cream blusher that we placed on the apples of Natasha's cheeks and brushed horizontally towards her hairline. This gave her face a softer, less angular look.

## HAIR

Natasha's hair was very long. The ends looked thin so we cut it to the shoulders for a softer, more voluminous look. By adding volume around Natasha cheeks we gave the illusion of plumping up her naturally thin face. We added a warm-coloured vegetable dye to Natasha's natural hair colour, which brought a soft hue to her complexion.

### WRINKLES AND FINE LINES

It is inevitable that over time you will notice that the number of fine lines and wrinkles on your face is increasing. This is partly to do with a change in hormones – a lessening of oestrogen, which keeps the skin supple – and partly just the wear and tear of living. If you have spent, or do still spend a lot of time in the sun, you will have far more, and deeper wrinkles than those people who stayed protected in the shade. Smoking is another habit that wreaks havoc on the skin. There are, however, a number of tips that help you to minimize the impact of the wrinkles or lines that you do have.

● The concealer you use to camouflage blemishes should be the same colour as your foundation.

● Apply concealer using a slightly damp brush. You will get more even coverage and more control than with the tip of your finger or an applicator.

● If you are self-concious about crowsfeet, use a bright blusher to draw attention away from the eyes. And use a good eye cream – it's a really worthwhile investment.

● To keep wrinkles from developing more quickly than necessary, remember to cleanse your face well, moisturize day and night, drink lots of water, exercise regularly and eat healthily.

# Belts

*A belt can make or break an outfit. Don't economise in this area. A belt has the same impact as a piece of jewellery and will last for years if you choose classic, neutral colours.*

Every wardrobe needs a minimum of two belts. One that is approximately 2cm (1in) wide and another approximately 4cm (2in) wide. The 2cm belt is perfect for trousers with narrow belt loops (usually found on smart, tailored trousers), the 4cm (2in) belt for casual chinos and jeans. Leather belts are the most practical and will last longer than those made from fabric. However, the focal point of every belt is the buckle. If you wear a lot of gold or silver, choose your metal buckle accordingly. Simple buckles work best. Avoid ornate designs and designer logos and initials. They date very quickly and the reason for buying designer pieces should be for the design of them, not the label. Luckily, most designers are now keeping their initials and logos to a discreet minimum, which is far more elegant. Some belts, particularly heavy ones, are made with detachable buckles so you can swop your buckle to suit your outfit.

**Choose the colour of your belt to go with your shoes if you want to draw attention to your waist and look co-ordinated.**

Choose the colour of your belt to match your shoes if you want to draw attention to your waist and look co-ordinated. If you don't want to over-define the waist area, then choose a belt in the same colour as your outfit. It is always a good idea to try on the belt you wish to buy with the garment you'll be wearing it with. Size is

important too. Although you can have extra holes punched into a belt that is too large, you don't want to have a long strip of extra leather hanging through the loop once you've done it up. A belt that is the right size should fasten in the middle hole. If you must shorten a belt, the ideal solution is to take it to a leather specialist who can shorten it from the buckle end. Start to collect a belt wardrobe, preferably in neutral colours that don't look too heavy so that you can wear then summer or winter, with light-weight or heavier fabrics. A choice eventually of four to six belts in your wardrobe will probably be sufficient. Those shown above and opposite are good examples.

**Tip:** In my experience, belts worn around the waist on anything but a pair of trousers or a skirt are an absolute no-no. Belts worn around your middle over a dress (whether the belt is made from leather or elastic) are extremely unflattering because they "cut" the body in half. They should be avoided regardless of whether they are in fashion or not.

## A belt that is the right size should fasten in the middle hole.

# Bags & Briefcases

*Even the most functional bag says lots about you. Your day bag is literally the wrapper on your work, reflecting your attitude to presentation. Look after your bag – scruffy bags, like clothes, give a bad impression.*

By polishing your bag regularly putting it on the floor as little as possible, where it can be scratched easily, you will find that a classic leather bag will last you several years.

## DAY BAGS

The working wardrobe needs two bags: a large one (probably a briefcase) for your day-to-day work requirements and a smaller handbag for all your personal belongings. A handbag is not an accessory you will necessarily wish to change every season, therefore, it is wise (and economical) to buy it in a neutral shade and in a classic style. Brightly coloured handbags should be saved for holidays and summertime.

Although bags don't really date, the fabric does. Nylon, for example, the height of fashion in the early to mid-90s, now looks dated. Leather is the one fabric that doesn't date and so is your most sensible option.

**An increasing number of women complain of aches and pains in their shoulders and necks caused by carrying bags that are too heavy.**

Your handbag should be as compact as possible. Many women complain of aches and pains in their shoulders and necks caused by carrying bags that are too heavy. This is why I advocate carrying two bags: a small, light one, which you carry at all times, and a larger one, which once at the office shouldn't leave your desk area until the end of the day.

It's very important to consider your size and the fit of your clothes when choosing a bag. If you

**BAG 1**
This bag can double up as a small briefcase. It is good for travelling as it has shoulder straps and an outside pocket with a secure brass clasp, so tickets and passport are easily accessible for you but not for pickpockets. The main part of the bag fastens with large press studs so that the contents are protected.
*Size: (w) 31cm x (h) 30cm*

**BAG 2**
A smaller version of bag 1, this bag has shoulder straps and a strap fastening around the bag itself for extra security. It is a smart classic that doubles up for sporty or more formal occasions.
*Size: (w) 22cm x (h) 25cm*

**BAG 3**
This is a more classic formal bag that will never date. It can be carried by hand or on the shoulder and is better suited to skirt-suits than to trousers or informal clothing.
*Size: (w) 26cm x (h) 27cm*

**BAG 4**
This bag in patent leather is smaller and more dressy than the other bags. It has laminate handles and is suitable to be worn with light-weight fabrics. In the right colour, it could double up as an evening bag.
*Size: (w)19cm x (h)17cm*

are short, you will find that smaller bags are more in proportion to your size. If you carry a large bag, it will give the impression that you are being weighed down. Taller women (unless they are extremely tall when small bags tend to look a bit prissy) especially if they combined with a large roomy coat, need not worry too much about size. To give you an idea, on these pages I would suggest bags 2, 3, 4, 8, 9, 10 for shorter women and for very tall women, bags 1, 5, 6, 8, 9.

## EVENING BAGS

I have never believed in spending vast sums of money on evening bags. After all, they spend much of their time under your chair, out of sight while you dine with friends or colleagues. I find that a simple black clutch bag in a size large enough to accommodate a lipstick, keys, some coins, a pair of tights and a handkerchief, is the most useful style. Clutch bags tend to be more flattering than shoulder bags since the straps of shoulder bags can often ruin the line of a beautiful evening dress. If you do wish to wear a shoulder bag in the evening it must be fashionable. This can serve as a useful way of dressing up a very plain dress. However, if you wear a flamboyant

**BAGS 5, 6, 7**
Above: This sturdy briefcase takes business folders and equipment, yet is feminine and elegant.
*Size: (w) 44cm x (h) 33cm*

Above right: This squashy, multizipped bag is useful for business-travel. A pocket under the flap hides items such as jewellery. The outside, zipped pocket can conceal travel tickets, purse, mobile phone, etc. Everything is easy for you to get at but difficult for others. This bag has been popular with fashion editors for some years.
*Size: (w) 38cm x (h) 29cm*

Below: This is a handy overnight bag that can double up as a sports bag. When it is is very full, it can be carried by hand.
*Size: (w) 51cm x (h) 19cm*

bag with a sparkling, patterned or intricately beaded dress, you could be in danger of overkill.

## BRIEFCASES

A classic large bag or briefcase should be roomy enough to carry everything you need – from folders to a spare pair of shoes. It doesn't necessarily need to be in the same material as your shoes but the colour should coordinate with the predominant neutrals in your wardrobe. If you're only going to invest in one briefcase, black is probably your safest bet. (Marks and scuffs are much easier to polish away on black leather than those on brown or tan leather.) Good briefcases are expensive but will last you for several years and

**BAG 8**
This unstructured leather handbag has a contrasting, coloured detail on the handle. It has a sporty look and the interesting design will jazz up a classic outfit. Worn on the shoulder or in the hand, it looks good with trouser suits.
*Size: (w) 25cm x (h) 27cm*

**BAG 9**
This is a structured leather bag with shoulder/hand strap. It looks very stylish with a dressy outfit and the shape looks good in other fabrics as well. The structured base means that it can stand easily.
*Size: (w) 26cm x (h) 23cm*

**BAG 10**
This evening bag can be changed into a clutch bag by detaching the strap. It is a young, modern shape and looks good in leather or fabric. Despite the gussetting, its contents should be kept to a minimum.
*Size: (w) 27cm x (h) 10cm*

will probably be used every day. Take a deep breath and think of it as investment dressing! They do have a language of their own and say a lot about you.

I like soft briefcases that are large enough to carry all your working day's requirements. They do not have to have the heavy frames and sharp angles of men's briefcases but do make sure that they have enough pockets for you to be organized and that they are not too heavy. If your case is heavy, make sure that you always bend from the knees when you pick it up, in order to avoid back strain.

**Tip:** Regard the appearance of your briefcase as part and parcel of your professional packaging. It will reflect your attitude to its contents. All bags should be cleaned and, if leather, they should be polished regularly. Above all, avoid that travesty of elegant presentation – a plastic carrier bag with your files in it!

> Good briefcases are expensive but will last you for several years and will probably be used every day. Take a deep breath and think of it as investment dressing!

# Glasses

*Glasses change your look and may affect the way you see yourself. As a result, it is very important that you buy the frame that makes you feel the most attractive.*

Until fairly recently, the choice of frames available was very poor and led more than one female to dispense with their specs and gaze hopefully, and myopically, into the distance in an attempt to focus on the world before them. The choice is wide enough now that everyone should be able to find something that they feel happy wearing.

### FINDING A PAIR TO SUIT

The frame of your glasses should not only relate to the shape of your face, it should also complement your clothes. If your face is square or round, or your features are very angular, do not reiterate these lines and shapes in your choice of frames. If the bridge of your glasses is high then this will accentuate a long nose. If your eyebrows protrude above the rim of your glasses, you may look as though you are in a permanent state of surprise.

If you have delicate colouring, strong black and coloured frames can look very harsh and are likely to detract from your facial features. My advice is to go to a reputable optician – a real pro who you can trust. Most good opticians will advise you according to your budget, face shape and hairstyle.

The style of frames changes from year to year and you may find that your choice appears limited. Do not despair, each frame will be slightly different. Don't buy anything that makes you feel plain – keep looking until you find a pair that you like. If you wish to minimize the impact of your glasses, you might consider a pair that has no frame at all. Leave time to choose your

> The frame of your glasses should not only relate to the shape of your face, it should also complement your clothes.

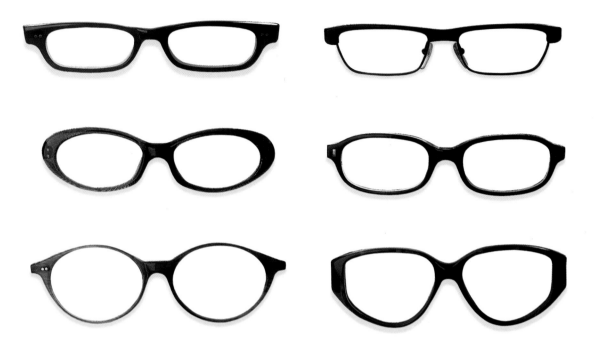

121

frames so that you are completely happy with your choice. Budget permitting, you may like to consider having two pairs of glasses. This is useful if one pair becomes damaged and, if you choose slightly different styles, is more interesting, allowing you to have different looks – a tortoiseshell pair, for example, for casual day- and office-wear, and for evening occasions, dressier gold- or silver-coloured frames that you can match with your accessories.

## SUNGLASSES

Aside from style, sunglasses are essential for shielding the delicate skin around the eyes, which is the area most susceptible to wrinkles. They should be worn all year,because even in winter or on dull days, harsh, damaging light and harmful rays are still present. Spend as much as you can afford on quality lenses and classic frames and, of course, they can be made up with prescription lenses.

**Tip:** It is worth shopping around for your frames – many opticians have sales, which can include stylish designer frames by companies such as Giorgio Armani and Calvin Klein.

**GLASSES SELECTION**
Although these frames all look very similar at first glance, you will find when you try them on that one pair suits you better than others. A slight difference in colour, the width of the rim and bridge and the style of the arms will all have an effect on your choice and give your face a different dimension.

# Scarves & Hats

*Scarves and hats are remarkably practical items, intended to keep us warm. But like everything else they, too, come in and out of fashion and can make or break an outfit.*

The wearing of scarves tends to follow current fashion trends. Depending on the style, they can be worn indoors and out and are worn increasingly with suits. Not only are they pretty accessories, but can take the place of jewellery and are a practical (and inexpensive) way of bringing colour to a neutral-coloured outfit. On a practical note, they also prevent recently applied make-up from marking the inside collar of your jacket and are far less expensive to dry clean than a suit. Silk, chiffon and other light scarves can be tied in a number of different ways, as illustrated (right) with both suit jackets and with coats.

For outdoor wear on summer evenings, large, fine cashmere or angora scarves and stoles are ideal for keeping your shoulders warm and can look extremely stylish with an evening dress.

**Tip:** Headscarves go in and out of fashion but, unless you're a movie star wishing to remain anonymous, never wear a scarf wrapped around the head and tied under the chin. It is one of fashion's most disastrous looks!

## HATS

You will always be noticed in a hat. Hats are either practical – keeping you warm in cold weather (we lose a lot of body heat through our heads) – or stylish confections to match an outfit for a special occasion.

The popularity of hats depends on how formally people are dressing at a particular time and on current hairstyle trends. Very full hairdos, for instance, do not show hats off to their best advantage. The proportions must be right. Short, neat haircuts or long hair that has been pinned up, look best with hats. Some styles – the beret, for example, which is not structured – look good with long, straight hair. Always consider your body proportions when choosing a hat – a small woman will be dwarfed by a large, wide-brimmed hat just as a pillbox hat will look too small on a large woman.

## You are best buying a hat in the base colour of your wardrobe so that you can wear it with either a suit or coat.

On a limited budget, you are best buying a hat in the base colour of your wardrobe so that you can wear it with either a suit or coat. If you're going to a wedding or special occasion and you're trying to buy a hat to match an outfit, it is essential to take the outfit along with you. If you are ever having trouble matching hat to outfit, ask a milliner to dress up a natural straw hat by adding a trimming in the appropriate colour. Although hats are less common than they used to be, don't be nervous and self-conscious about wearing them – they can look marvellous.

123

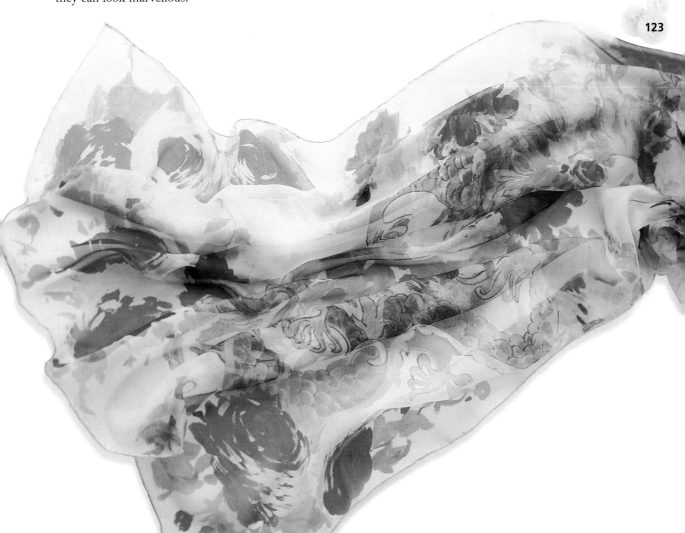

# Makeover *Barbara*

Barbara works from an office although her job requires her to meet clients from time to time. Like her product, she must look up-to-the-minute, but her employers enforce no strict dress code.

### BEFORE

Before her makeover, Barbara wore round glasses and had a short haircut with a severe fringe. The fringe made her face look shorter than it needed to and the glasses hid even more of her face. A loose, unstructured shirt and cardigan that came to about hip level cut her body at the worst point and this, coupled with her flat lace-ups, emphasized her lack of height.

### WHAT WE DECIDED TO DO

It was important to give Barbara more height, help to improve her posture and "stand tall", to "open up" her face and to change her glasses.

## VITAL STATISTICS

Barbara Waters
**Age:** 36
**Height:** 4ft 11in
**Dress size:** 10/12
**Occupation:** Marketing Executive in Computer Software Company
**Aim:** To project a stylish, trendy image, suitable for office wear and seeing clients.

> '*I love my new look – I hadn't realized what a difference a new pair of specs and a haircut could make.*'
>
> BARBARA

### CLOTHES

We needed to dress Barbara fashionably in clothes that could take her anywhere. Her leather trousers are a straight-leg cut (flattering to the thighs) and can be worn with or without a jacket, depending on the formality of the occasion. For the evening, they can be dressed up with a glamorous top and higher heels

## We deliberately chose a low-cut neckline to make her neck seem longer

that would also give Barbara more height. We chose a straight black cardigan edged in grey – an original design that would reflect Barbara's some creativity and awareness of fashion trends. We deliberately chose a low-cut, V-shaped neckline to make her neck seem longer. The shoulders of the cardigan were (turn to p. 126)

**NECKLINE** Now Barbara's hair is softer and lighter and she has smaller glasses and softly padded shoulders, a feature can be made of her shoulders and neckline. The dual colour adds a neat, uncluttered note of interest.

**CUFFS** Rather than using jewellery, the matching collar and cuff details added a strong, contemporary feel.

**HAT** Accessorizing with a squashy hat – easy to wear with short hair – gives the outfit a casual, weekend look.

**BOOTS** This chunky, high heeled leather boot gives length to the leg, continuous unbroken lines and as much height as Barbara can comfortably handle.

**125**

**LEATHER** Used for day or evening, leather is a comfortable, sympathetic fabric, suitable for summer and winter.

slightly padded, which offset Barbara's tendency towards sloping shoulders and created a squarer, stronger look. The length of the cardigan was all-important, ending just at the top of Barbara's thighs. This length, coupled with the long row of buttons down the front, streamlined her figure and was very slimming. Moreover, like most women, Barbara reacted to the more structured style of the clothing and the heeled boots by standing straighter, which automatically gave the impression of more height and of greater confidence.

## GLASSES

Barbara's former glasses were too round, sat too high on her face and drew attention to her full cheeks by echoing their curves. They also had thin, gold frames that didn't help her complexion. We decided to give her a trendy pair of tortoiseshell oval frames that flattered the shape and colour of her eyes and made her face look more slender.

## MAKE-UP

Barbara had slightly hooded eyes that needed to be defined. We shaded in her eyebrows and painted the

**Barbara had slightly hooded eyelids that needed defining.**

*' If you have slightly hooded eyes, avoid using dark shadow except at the edges of your eyelid. Otherwise, your eyelids will seem even heavier. '*

MAGGIE HUNT, MAKE-UP ARTIST

126

roots of her lashes to add definition and volume. We shaped her eyes upwards with a dark eyeshadow. On her lips, we put pearl lipstick and gloss.

## HAIR

Barbara's hair was already short but the hair on the top of her head was slightly flat. Therefore, we layered it and blow-dried it using the fingers to give it a natural lift. We gave Barbara an off-centre parting – always more flattering than a central one – and got rid of the heavy fringe. We left Barbara with a few strands that fell over her forehead without obliterating it completely. Losing the fringe and allowing her face to be seen right up to the hair line, lengthened and thinned her face and created a triangular shape that echoed her jaw and chin rather than her full cheeks.

We also decided to darken Barbara's natural hair colour as we thought it was a bit too blond for her complexion, making it look rather dull. We added a vegetable dye to darken the blond and combed highlights through the hair around the hair line to light up her face and draw attention to her eyes and browline.

### MAKING UP YOUR EYES

Your eyes, it is said, are the windows of your soul, so the way you make them up can speak volumes. Shadow comes in shades from soft and neutral to strong and bright. Eyeliners can be pencils or liquid put on with a brush. Decide whether you want to look natural or dramatic. You probably want to do both, depending on the occasion, where you are going and whom you are seeing. The main thing is to learn which colours and textures suit you and how to flatter the shape and colour of your eyes. A general rule is that eyeshadow that is too dark will make your eyes look smaller. Pale colours are more natural and open up the eyes if applied well. To make shadow last, brush your lid with loose powder before applying the shadow. If you cover them with foundation, your eyeshadow will crease.

### EYE SHAPES

● For hooded eyelids, use a neutral, darkish shadow at the corner of the eyes. Avoid colour in the centre of the lids as this will make them look heavier. Using eyelash curlers also helps to minimize heavy lids.

● Small eyes benefit from light, shimmery, neutral tones that help to "open them up".

● For prominent eyes, use dark shadow, extending beyond the natural crease of the eyelid.

● For close-set eyes, define only the outer edges of the lid to make your eyes seem further apart. Shadow under the eye will also give more width between them.

● For wide-set eyes, cover the whole lid with a narrow band of shadow.

# How to Shop

❖

*Effective shopping is an art that ensures
you have the right wardrobe for your
personality and lifestyle, with the minimum of
fuss. It is an art that most of us have to learn,
so never be afraid to ask for help.*

# Shopping

*Very often we buy clothes impulsively and with little forethought. For the busy woman, shopping can be a nightmare of rushing from shop to shop, desperately looking for something suitable.*

In this situation, she usually ends up buying for short-term use only. In this chapter I intend to point out some of the hazards and pitfalls of shopping, explain how the retail trade works, and help you to develop a few essential "shopping skills".

### SHOPPING MISTAKES

The most common mistake is to shop without a list. If you are to buy a few clothes but of a very high quality, then cost, planning and analysis are vital. Use the list of clothes that remain after your wardrobe "edit" (see p. 99) whenever you shop. If you use its details of cut, cloth and colour and ask yourself the questions on these pages, you should never be tempted to make an unwise purchase.

Many women buy clothes on impulse – often when they need cheering up. This is when horrific mistakes can be made. If you tend to be impulsive, acknowledge the tendency and rather than buy a garment that will make you feel guilty afterwards, buy something less extravagant like make-up or perfume. Even a good hair conditioner or a bottle of scented body lotion can give you a boost, whereas an expensive blouse that you only wear once would be sheer folly. Remember the cost-per-wear theory; if you use that body lotion for two months, it has been a far more economical investment than the once-worn blouse. Save your clothes shopping for a time when you feel calm, logical and happy!

Newspapers and magazines sometimes influence us to buy clothes that we should not even be thinking about! Every woman's magazine has a fashion section, as do most newspapers, and the clothes that they show are invariably worn by very young, tall, thin professional models who bear little resemblance to the majority of us. What they look good in will not necessarily look good on the

**Many women buy clothes on impulse usually at times when they need cheering up and this is when horrific mistakes can be made.**

## THE CUT

- Does it fit me?
- How does it move?
- Does the shape flatter me?
- Is the cut soft or sharp?
- Do the details show a strong fashion influence?
- Can it be altered?
- Will it be wearable in two years' time?
- Do I feel comfortable in it?

130

' *Fashion should indicate a way of thinking, not just a way of dressing.* '

GIORGIO ARMANI, FASHION DESIGNER

average – even the above average – woman. If you relied on the fashion pages, you could end up believing that when a "new look" takes off, that it is the only one available. Remember that the media always seeks the sensational and a "new look" can happily fill column inches. Realism, however, is seldom newsworthy, and the shops still stocking realistic clothes are not always likely to be the ones that receive exposure. Consider too, that fashion companies often use PRs to get publicity, and that being written about is not necessarily a recommendation of quality. Realistically, therefore, most media fashion coverage doesn't help women to choose clothes that really suit them as individuals. What you can learn from good fashion pages is how to put a "look" together and what accessories work best with different styles of clothing.

## ASKING FOR ASSISTANCE

Most clothes shops gear themselves to selling to a particular sort of customer, described in terms of age, income and quality preference. So be prepared when you walk into a good-quality clothes shop for an instant judgement to be made about you. We all know the sort of shops where, if you look a mess, sales staff might just ignore you. You don't have to dress up in your smartest clothes, but if you don't look scruffy, they'll think you're a serious customer. If you wish to pre-empt any judgement, just walk in and ask for advice immediately. You may find it difficult – many people dislike displaying that lack of confidence – but it could be absolutely the right thing to do. In my experience, the women who ask for advice are the ones who are actually more knowledgeable about fashion because they are very aware of what they don't know and are keen to learn. The customer who comes in saying "I know exactly what suits me", is generally the one who needs the most help because she is stuck in a fashion rut. Fashion moves forward and so should she.

### THE CLOTH

● Is the weight appropriate for the temperature in which I work/travel/socialize?

● Does it feel soft or stiff?

● How does it fit in with other fabrics in my wardrobe?

● Is it easily cleaned?

● Does it need to be lined?

● Will it crease easily?

● How do I care for it?

**131**

### THE COLOUR

● How does it fit in with the rest of my wardrobe?

● Does it suit me?

● Will I get tired of it?

● Will it show dirt easily?

● Will it be difficult to match?

● Is it a particularly strong fashion colour?

● Do I feel good in it?

● Will I need to buy new accessories as well?

## SHOP ASSISTANTS

The perfect sales person should be a sartorial psychologist with a good sense of style, proportion and colour who can tune into you and your lifestyle fairly rapidly. She should be able to make a quick assessment of your shape and suggest items from her stock that will suit you. Knowledge of stock is vital for skilled selling and should include accessories and shoes, although these may need to be sourced at another shop.

> If you feel pressured into buying something against your better judgement, tell the assistant that you will think about it and return.

Being uncertain about what suits you or what you want is a major shopping problem and you could fall victim to a forceful sales person. If you feel pressured into buy something against your will, say you will think about it and return. The asistant's reaction should be a barometer to her integrity. If she takes issue, then the item may not really suit you. If she's amenable, then her judgement is probably sound. However, if you've absorbed the lessons of this book, you should be more confident in your own instincts. Always be honest with the assistant. If she says that you look marvellous, but you can't see it, then tell her. Ask her to be more precise about cut, cloth, colour, fit etc., and respond. Shopping is a two-way process and involves communication between customer and assistant. It would be a mistake to grumble if your input had not been entirely truthful.

Finally, never buy clothes in a hurry. This is when the greatest mistakes can be made. Take time to try clothes on and never let an assistant hurry you. Move about in the garment as you would at home or at work. If you sit a lot, then sit in the clothes in the shop to ensure they are comfortable. Look at yourself in the mirrors from all angles and ask for another if necessary to see back and sides properly. Only when you are absolutely sure, should you say "yes".

## WHERE TO SHOP

When going clothes shopping, there are roughly three different types of shop to choose from – designer boutiques, department stores and high-street shops. Each type has its own "style" and its devoted customers. It's up to you to decide which shops are most suited to you. There is no doubt that fashion shops have an identity.

132

### IDENTIFYING A "GOOD" SHOP

First of all, customers need to be aware that not all the fashion industry's practices are above reproach. Did you know for instance, that some shops use mirrors with a slimming effect or that others use special music to lull you into a spending mood? Word of mouth (a tip from someone whose opinion you trust) is usually the best recommendation of all. Also, new shops often take a while to establish their style and to determine exactly what sort of customer they appeal to. So if you want reliable advice, you're better off going to a shop that has already carved a niche for itself and which understands its customers. A good shop will have a good reputation.

Before you even walk into a shop, you more or less know the kind of clothes you're going to find.

Designer boutiques are at the top end of the market. Some carry one designer exclusively e.g. Chanel or Ralph Lauren, but you can expect greater choice in a shop that carries several labels.

If you want to buy designer clothes, comb the market to find out who designs for your lifestyle. Fashion magazines and advertisements can be useful in this respect. In my opinion, some designers have been "hyped" to a level out of proportion with their talent. The best

*' Women are not dolls to be dressed by designers; I would ask them, have you no brains? Yes, you have intelligence. Then please express that intelligence in dressing yourself. ,*

JEAN PATOU, FASHION DESIGNER

designers, however, have often been around for years and have a faithful following. Their clothes will not date and, if cared for, should last for years. I prefer Italian design for women's business wear – the cut and cloth tend to be of excellent quality and are more feminine. For casual wear, Italian and American designers can't be beaten. If you want casual wear in really exquisite fabrics, the Italians do it best. American designers are unsurpassed in really functional, hard-wearing casuals.

A suit from a quality, designer shop will never be cheap and if you really cannot afford such an investment I still urge you to visit these shops to study the clothes. Learn what makes their merchandise such high quality in terms of cut, cloth and colour and use this knowledge to discriminate when you are shopping on the high street. However, be warned: "quality" is highly addictive! I suggest that as soon as you are in an income bracket where you can afford to buy one designer outfit for a season rather than several cheaper ones (even if it is only at sale time) you really should. It will be a good investment.

Browsing in designer shops can give a fascinating insight into how the fashion industry works. If you pop into a high-street store afterwards, you will, in all probability, see the adapted versions of the designers' trends. To keep costs down, however, the high-street versions will have been mass produced in cheaper fabrics and cut and cloth may well be incompatible. A figure-hugging number skilfully cut by the designer in a soft wool jersey, will have been cut in a more extreme way and in a cheaper fabric by the designers working for high-street chains, and probably won't work at all in the way the original designer intended.

**134**

> ' *Fashion is a form of ugliness so intolerable that we have to alter it every six months.* '
> OSCAR WILDE, WRITER

## WHEN TO SHOP

For some women, browsing in shops is very relaxing and shopping is almost a hobby. Many of us would like to have plenty of time to shop but end up doing it in a rushed and harassed state of mind. As I've already said, this is a basic shopping mistake. You will find shopping a more pleasant experience if you consider the best times

**Many of us would like to have plenty of time to shop but end up doing it in a rushed and harassed state of mind. This . . . is one of the most basic shopping mistakes.**

to go – both for yourself and for the shops. For instance, the best "spiritual" time to go is when you feel positive about yourself; if you are feeling negative, you won't be satisfied with anything that you see or try on.

Shops have the widest possible selection of stock around February/March and September/October, so if you can schedule major shopping trips to coincide with these times, you will have the optimum choice.

To assemble a complete outfit, it is often necessary to visit several shops, which is very time consuming if you do it on a piecemeal basis. (Mail order shopping is booming, as a result, although this has problems for women to whom a perfect fit and quality of cut and cloth is important.) You can use your shopping time much more effectively by having a couple of major buying sessions a year when you buy important items and complete outfits, rather than a steady "dribble" of purchases throughout the year. And if you are spending a lot of time scouring a small town for what you want, then you will be much better off making a day of it in a large city a couple of times a year.

Always avoid lunch times and Saturdays when shops are at their busiest. I like shopping in the morning when the sales staff tend to be fresh and (one hopes) helpful. If you are very busy yourself, you might like to shop by appointment – phoning the shop in advance so they can think about your requirements beforehand. Some shops will stay open late if you have made an appointment, making your shopping all the easier "out of hours".

## IN-STORE TAILORING

Some shops have access to a tailor and this can help since very few women find clothes that fit them exactly. I almost regard a sale as a "first fitting" before the necessary small alterations are made. Skirts and sleeves can be adjusted, waists and hips can be let out or, more easily, taken in – even the bust can be altered. Many shops that do not have an alterations facility try to persuade the customer that an ill-fitting garment actually fits well. If you are looking for a good fit, you can easily end up in despair at the irregularities in your shape. Take heart and remember that the garment is made in a fixed shape

---

### DON'T BELIEVE THE LABEL

Sizing varies enormously from manufacturer to manufacturer so you should never go shopping seeing yourself rigidly as one size. Many labels are deceptive and one designer might call you a size 12, another a size 10 or a 14. Avoid discounting garments because they don't seem to be your size – you could have a pleasant surprise when you try them on!

135

with a view to it fitting many different bodies. There is absolutely no reason why you should expect clothes to fit your body perfectly, and a skilled alterations person will be able to almost totally remake a garment. Of course, cost is a factor in all this and extensive alteration work to an already expensive suit could prove prohibitive. But if you really love a garment and want to feel completely comfortable in it, then it is definitely worth taking the time and spending the money to have it altered. It is an investment after all.

## How the Retail Business Works

Very few customers know how the retail trade works – just how far in advance a range of clothes is chosen, for instance – so I think an explanation might help you in refining your shopping skills.

In any one year, I go the Milan collections at the end of February to buy clothes for the following winter. This "buy" has to happen early because, at the more expensive end of the market, manufacturers only produce to order. The designers whose collections I see, will have visited the fabric shows the previous September/October and will have spent the five or six months in between creating their collections.

It comes as a surprise to many that, to a very large extent, it is the fabric manufacturers who dictate what we shall be wearing: if they produce fabrics that are more fluid, the designers cannot produce tailored clothes. If they decide that there have been enough black and browns, they will say we are ready for something else. If a lot of checks have been around, they might decide that we should go into spots or stripes. The fabric manufacturers, like any designer, have to sell their goods so are constantly having to come up with something new. They have a great deal of power.

... it is the fabric manufacturers who dictate what we shall be wearing: if they produce fabrics that are more fluid, the designers cannot produce tailored clothes.

### THE PROCESS

Once the designer has chosen the fabrics, he or she will produce design samples using those fabrics. The total fabric order will only be confirmed once the collection has been shown and the orders

' *How men hate waiting while the wives shop for clothes and trinkets, how women hate waiting, often for much of their lives, while their husbands shop for fame and glory.* '

THOMAS SZASZ, *THE SECOND SKIN*

collated. Some designers pre-buy fabrics – either for early delivery or for exclusivity – and it is always obvious as a buyer when they have done so, as the "selling" of the garments of this particular fabric is so keen! After these fabric orders have been confirmed in February, the fabrics are manufactured, the designs made up and Wardrobe could expect to see about half its February orders arriving in July, with the remainder in August/September. This is not very long for some very complicated processes (and there is many a slip between the time of the initial order and delivery).

Meanwhile, around April, (a few weeks after their current collection) the designers return to the fabric shows to see the fabrics for their collections for spring and summer of the following year. These we will see in the September/October again in Milan and we would expect delivery of completed clothes in about December or January.

## THE BUYER'S JOB

In Milan, there is a huge centre where there are perhaps 2000 stands on which designers show their wares; the clothes themselves are on rails or on mannequins. These stands show the cheaper *prêt à porter*, or "ready-to-wear", collections; the high fashion designers have their own showrooms. There are some designer showrooms I wouldn't be admitted to as I do not sell their clothes. For, in order to offer exclusivity, major designers only have one, two, perhaps three stockists in one city. This makes sense because in that price range, the customer doesn't want to bump into another identical suit or dress!

## BUYING CONSIDERATIONS

Once I see a collection that I like, I introduce myself and my company and find out about other stockists in London and whether

137

### SALES SHOPPING

Shops hold sales to help their cash flow and to sell unsold and sometimes ill-fitting stock. They are not always a boon for the customers. It is very easy at sale time to get carried away on a wave of adrenaline at the excitement of finding a bargain. But the shrewd sales shopper goes to a shop where she knows the stock, to buy something that she has wanted but not previously been able to afford. Try to avoid thinking about a new fashion garment all season, then succumbing to it "because it was cheap in the sale" and, ultimately, never wearing it. Also, don't be seduced into buying things that you don't need just because they are reduced. Really scan your wardrobe list before you go to the sales. It is always a good idea to ask your favourite shop to mail you about the first day of their sale. More often than not there is a preview day for mailing-list customers.

they can supply me. Then I look around and try the clothes on –
I need to see if they can work on an average-size woman. I start to
buy, bearing in mind the characteristics and sizes of my customers.
I think about the shapes, what colours I sell well, what the garments
look like, who will buy them, how many of each I should buy, what
fabrics the garments will look best in and the price.

This moment is critical to my business and it can be very traumatic.
If I buy too many of one garment, they won't all sell and capital is
tied up; if I buy too few, I may lose out by not having enough of a
popular style; if the colour or fabric is wrong, the clothes won't sell.
You must not be carried away by media hype, salesmanship or sheer
passion. You are committed once an order is placed and signed for,
and the designers are under no obligation to accept a cancellation.

As we order from one designer, we must consider what we've
ordered elsewhere. We keep a log and every evening list the day's
buying into how many coats, skirts, dresses, etc. so that we can see
the ratio of dresses to jackets etc. and work out whether we have
enough top and bottom halves. It's rather like assembling a jigsaw!
The colours must be right too, in terms of what the customers like
and what is fashionable - but also for the shop. If too many colours
are thrown together haphazardly, the shop itself will look a mess.

## AND YOU THOUGHT IT WAS GLAMOROUS!

The clothes ordered in February will begin to arrive in July with the
bulk coming in September. If a collection is late, a shop could be
virtually empty of stock during an important selling period. Delays
are endemic in the fashion business: if there are flaws in the fabrics
garments will be sent back; if there is a lorry, train or port authority
strike, we're stymied; if buttons are not delivered on time, whole
collections can be sitting there, unable to be delivered.

Once the clothes do arrive, there can still be problems – jackets
might arrive without matching bottoms so they cannot be sold until
they do arrive, for example. I remember when we once had to return
silk suits that had top and bottom halves from different dye lots –
leaving us lacking 36 suits that we'd raved about to our customers.

Another problem – perhaps the worst one – is that merchandise
can differ from the original sample. We try on samples when we

### A SUCCESSFUL COLLECTION

Once the clothes come into the shops, our customers are informed by letter or telephone and we place advertisements in the national press. If our buying has been intelligent, the clothes will walk off the racks and we can congratulate ourselves on having bought a successful collection. If our buying included some risk factors – something really unusual, or extremely expensive – they might take longer to sell but I would still want to buy them if they are really stunning. Otherwise I would end up with a shop full of very, very safe merchandise and I don't think that's what my customers necessarily want. Even though the suit they buy is for work, they like to be up to the minute and they certainly don't want to be bored.

talk to designers in order to check that the garment "works". If we think there is a flaw, we place our order on condition that they rectify it before the stock is delivered. For the same reason, we try the clothes on again when they arrive in the shop. This is how we once discovered that a collar rise on a jacket was an inch higher than it had been on the sample. If we hadn't tried the jacket, we would have lost sales, simply because the collar was uncomfortable. Those slightly misshapen clothes you are always seeing in shop sales, are manufacturers' errors which the buyer didn't pick up.

## Those slightly misshapen clothes you are always seeing in shop sales, are manufacturers' errors which the buyer didn't pick up.

# Travelling

*Travelling is tiring and usually involves discomfort and hassle. Be prepared for a great deal of walking, and for cramped, uncomfortable seating arrangements.*

Whoever said "It is better to travel in anticipation than to arrive," never experienced today's travelling problems – delays, rush-hours, miles of airport walkways.

## BUSINESS TRAVEL

If you travel on business regularly, packing can become a chore. It is often dreaded and inevitably done in a rush, usually the night before. I try to make a list of things I must remember to pack the weekend before to save me forgetting small items such as my tweezers, a piece of jewellery I want to wear to a dinner or a special belt.

**Keep your travelling wardrobe to a minimum so you can spend your business trip concentrating on just that — business.**

When packing for a business trip, efficiency and an immaculate appearance should be your main priorities. Whereas when packing for a holiday, looking glamorous and pampering yourself is a more important consideration.

### YOUR BUSINESS WARDROBE

For a business trip, build your wardrobe around a basic colour. If you are going on a four-day trip, travelling on two days and attending a conference on the remaining two, then you could pack two suits (one in black and one in grey or navy) that go with black shoes and black briefcase. If it is summer and you're wearing brown shoes, a cream, tan or soft green suit would be practical and would save you doubling up on accessories. Add a couple of sweaters, T-shirt-style tops or blouses depending on the time of year. Tops can transform an outfit and they are light and easy to pack.

Remember, the more you take, the more time you will spend deciding what to wear. Keep your travelling wardrobe to a minimum so that you can spend your business trip concentrating on just that – business. Mix and match in the following way:

### JEWELLERY

You needn't take a lot of jewellery when you travel. Taking too much is often a hindrance because you'll worry about where you've left it and whether it is safe. If you travel wearing a pair of smart yet discreet earrings (pearl studs, for example), you should only need one other pair for evenings and, perhaps, a necklace. Taking a whole box of trinkets is unwise and unnecessary.

'*Any man can be in good spirits and good temper when he's well dressed.*'

CHARLES DICKENS, NOVELIST

DAY 1: To travel, wear suit A, ready for your meeting, with a sweater and a coat or raincoat. Note that an overcoat can be a real burden when you are travelling. Wearing warmer clothes and a wind-resistant, light-weight raincoat is often more practical.

DAY 2: For your first conference day, wear suit B with a sweater, blouse or good quality T-shirt in the day. Wear suit A in evening with a different blouse or dressy top. Change jewellery.

DAY 3: Wear suit A in day, adding a scarf instead of jewellery and suit B in the evening with a different blouse or top from day 2 and different jewellery.

DAY 4: Wear suit B with a fine sweater and coat or raincoat.

## HOW TO PACK

Always put tailored clothes at the bottom of the suitcase. Never carry them in a soft, frameless bag as they will crumple. Roll T-shirts and lingerie and put them, with your shoes (which should be in a cloth bag and have shoe trees to protect their shape) around the edges. Carry your washbag in another bag so there is no risk of spillage. Because I travel a lot, I keep a wash-bag ready to travel with a set of small bottles containing my skin-care products. A toothbrush, toothpaste and a moisturiser in a make-up bag is a good idea when travelling long distances in economy class.

### HOW TO FOLD CLOTHES

To fold a jacket, button it up, fold it in two across the body, reveres facing you, and bring the arms across the chest. Use tissue paper or polythene to pad any obvious places where creasing will occur like the shoulders and reveres. Apply the same principle to dresses, shirts and trousers.

**SCARVES**

Scarves are useful accessories. I love to travel with a pashmina shawl, which keeps me really warm in the plane and which looks great worn around the shoulders in the evening.

**141**

EXTRAS WORTH TAKING

There are always extra small things that you may need, or wish to take with you. This is a list of the things that I always take with me.

- Hairdryer. Although most hotels provide them, I prefer to use my own. Don't forget an adaptor plug if you're going abroad.
- Shoe creams. Hotels usually provide shoe shine, but they rarely provide creams in the right colours.
- A mini-repair kit with safety pins, needles and thread that matches the contents of your travelling wardrobe
- A telescopic umbrella
- A small clothes brush – preferably the type with a velour panel.
- A special beauty treatment – a face-mask, for example – that I might have more time for away from home.
- An exercise gadget (e.g. resistance bands) or a list of exercises so that I can keep up a routine while away.
- Bath oils. I always travel with one that is relaxing and another that wards off colds and flu.

## WHAT TO WEAR WHEN YOU TRAVEL

Comfort must be the main priority when deciding what to travel in. Many years ago I would have suggested a tracksuit but these days I would no longer feel comfortable doing so. Instead, I would probably wear a pair of Lycra-mix stretch trousers because they don't crease much, with a cardigan or a knitted two-piece, which is a smarter, modern version of the tracksuit. Wearing comfortable shoes is vital. Feet often swell on aeroplanes and delayed take-off and connections can sometimes result in you wearing your shoes for much longer than planned. If you're travelling to a hot destination, it's worth packing a sarong and a T-shirt in your hand luggage so that you can change just before landing. This way, you won't suffer in the heat on arrival at your destination.

**Comfort must be the main priority when choosing what to wear for travelling.**

## LUGGAGE

One of the first considerations should be your luggage. It is often more important than you think, especially when you are being picked up by a business colleague. Much as we hate to admit it,

### TRAVEL-FRIENDLY FABRICS

Light-weight fabrics and those combined with Lycra travel well and crease minimally. In summer, if you decide to take a linen suit, take a portable steam iron with you or check that the hotel has a good pressing facility. It's always a good idea to plan to get your clothes cleaned just before you go away. Then you can pack them in the cleaner's polythene bags – these are more efficient than tissue paper in keeping creases at bay. Do be careful with polythene bags with names and logos printed on to them. Should moisture seep into your suitcase, you may find your suit suddenly bearing the name of your local dry-cleaner!

we are judged as much by what we carry as by what we wear. Hotel porters, for instance, often treat you differently if you have good luggage rather than a tattered case. Presumably, if you look expensive and the luggage enhances the hotel foyer, it makes you a prestigious guest.

I like nylon-canvas luggage; it is light and hard wearing. You can build up a luggage "wardrobe" comprising a large suitcase, then a piece of hand luggage, and perhaps a suit carrier. Soft luggage can have an attractive leather trim and if you buy it with a frame it will protect your clothes as well. Although good luggage is expensive, it should last. My suitcase has lasted for 10 years and although it will soon need replacing, it has travelled many, many miles and was a worthwhile investment. In my experience, cheap luggage will not stand the wear and tear of aeroplane holds. No one envies the poor passenger who on reaching their destination finds an open suitcase and half their laundry circling the carousel.

As an alternative, fibreglass suitcases are hard wearing. They often come with sets of wheels, which are useful if you have to walk down endless corridors at the airport. Always label your luggage very carefully and if you have a suitcase that is a popular make, it's worth adding a distinguishing mark to avoid confusion when collecting your luggage from the carousel. There is nothing worse after a long journey than discovering that your luggage has been taken by somebody else who mistook it for their own.

**Tip:** Always take the weight of an empty suitcase into consideration before buying; you don't want to buy something that you have difficulty lifting when empty, let alone full.

## HEALTH AND BEAUTY TRAVEL CARE

Looking good when you arrive at the airport is one thing, looking (and feeling) good once you've reached your destination is quite another. By following a few simple guidelines you should be able to minimize the negative effects of flying.

• Always pack a good facial moisturiser in your hand luggage. On a long haul flight, it's worth applying every few hours to combat the dehydrating effects of a long journey. A facial spray (my favourite is Evian) can be very refreshing.

**143**

**TIPS**

● I find it useful to decant some of my washing detergent into a small bottle, which I put into my wash bag. Travel washes I've tried are rarely as efficient as my own.

● If I am going abroad, I always transfer my English money into a spare purse, which avoids complications and is a useful device for maintaining good relations with cab drivers!

' *When visiting hotels, it's wrong to assume that someone will always whip-up an ironing board when you need it ...* ,

GLENYS ROBERTS, WRITER AND NEWSPAPER COLUMNIST

- To reduce the effects of jet lag on the day of my return I set my watch to British time on waking and eat accordingly. If I were flying from America to Britain, I'd eat lunch in the morning and have my equivalent of an evening meal in the early afternoon. Early evening I would just have a light snack. This system minimizes the effects of air travel on my "body clock". Some airlines are flexible in their catering arrangements and will readily provide a vegetarian meal or fruit plate if asked.

- You will feel much better after a long flight if you avoid alcohol, drink lots of water and eat fruit instead of salty snacks and nuts.

- Joints often become stiff and feet and ankles can swell during flights. Gentle exercise (stretching, rotating the ankles and head, lifting the shoulders and taking the occasional walk down the aisle) will help to combat swollen limbs and stiffness.

- To help you sleep, take an eye mask and an inflatable neck cushion. Half inflated, they are very comfortable and make snoozing easy.

- Air travel can be stressful and tiring so go as comfortably as you can afford. You might think that it's a needless extravagance to travel business class, but your performance at the other end will undoubtedly benefit from a journey that is as comfortable and as stress-free as possible. In travel, as in all things, be kind to yourself!

## WHAT TO DO BEFORE YOU TRAVEL

- If you travel a lot, thinking about your hair and make-up is important. For instance, if you travel to hot climates a great deal, it makes sense to have your hair pulled or gelled back away from the face to keep cool. High maintenance hair requiring many combs and clips just isn't practical. It's always worth visiting a good hairdresser who can give you an easy-to-maintain stylish cut – what I call "wash and wear" hair.

You will feel much better after a long flight if you avoid alcohol, drink plenty water and eat fruit, instead of salty snacks and nuts.

• If your hair is coloured, plan a visit to the hairdresser well in advance so that you don't have to spend hours in a salon at the last minute when you have a host of other things to think about and do.

• If you're going on a summer holiday and will be exposing your feet and toes, make an appointment to see a chiropodist and have a pedicure. Sea water, sand and chlorine can often cause nail polish to chip so it's always worth taking a bottle of nail polish remover and a bottle of the nail colour used with you.

• However cumbersome they are, it's worth taking a good selection of sun-protection and after-sun products when travelling to a hot destination. The quality of sun creams abroad vary and you may not find the level of protection you need.

• Many of us rarely find the time to pamper ourselves at home. Holidays are the perfect opportunity to do this so take your favourite lotions, potions and masks with you and indulge! (For more information on hair and make-up see pp. 24–28.)

## HOLIDAY TRAVEL

For a one-week beach holiday, I would suggest that you pack:

2 swimsuits (1 in black that can be used under a sarong for evening)

2 sarongs; 1 long skirt

1 sun dress; 2 pairs summer trousers; 1 pair shorts

1 smart dress for evening

1 cardigan; 1 lightweight sweater

1 beach hat; 1 pair thong sandals (or similar); 1 pair gym shoes

1 pair of sandals suitable for the day and smarter evening wear

an assortment of tops including white T-shirts and 1 loose, white linen shirt

lingerie; 1 pair sunglasses; 1 belt.

For a week in the city, my list would be as follows:

1 skirt suit (the colour and fabric depending on the climate)

1 pair matching trousers

1 dress (to co-ordinate with the suit jacket)

1 less formal jacket

T-shirts; 2 sweaters or tops; 2 blouses

2 pairs of shoes (one for day for walking, one for evening)

lingerie; 1 belt; 1 pair sunglasses

### A LUST FOR LISTS

My husband is forever teasing me about my passion for list making! I find writing lists the single most efficient way of staying focused in the different areas of my life and yes, if I could pass on only one piece of advice to other women, it would be to write lists! They are particularly useful when travelling. Start one well in advance when you have a quiet moment and note everything from "Pearl earrings" and "Cancel the newspapers" to "Adapter plug", "Buy bikini" and "Book leg waxing". Closer to the departure date you may wish to subdivide this list into: "What to buy from the pharmacy" or "What to pack" until every task is completed. By being organized you will feel in control and dramatically reduce your stress levels.

**145**

By being organized you will feel in control.

# Clothes Care

*If you want to look well groomed, wardrobe maintenance is a must. Your clothes and accessories will last longer and you will save time because everything in your wardrobe will be ironed, cleaned and ready to wear.*

To keep clothes in top-notch condition, have a weekly wardrobe check – on a Sunday night perhaps. Cast your eye over your clothes, shoes and bags and decide what needs cleaning, mending or pressing. This need only take half an hour and you can go to work on Monday morning knowing that you are "well maintained" for the week ahead!

## SORTING

Hang clothes up as soon as you take them off and put them somewhere to air before returning them to the wardrobe. Creases will fall out of most fabrics if the garment still retains heat from your body. Don't leave things in the pockets because this pulls the garment out of shape. Give your clothes a good brush to remove bits of dust and fluff that might have accumulated during the day. An outfit in a plain fabric will always need brushing because it will show specks more clearly than patterned fabric. Velcro-type material pads are more efficient in removing fluff than traditional bristle brushes.

**Hang clothes up as soon as you take them off and put them somewhere to air before returning them to the wardrobe.**

Hang up all your clothes apart from sweaters, T-shirts and lingerie. Store in the wardrobe with enough space between garments so that they do not crumple. Wire coat hangers can damage shoulder lines and are too insubstantial for most outfits, so use chunky wooden or plastic ones. I find that hanging trousers from the waist (rather than folding them over a bar) is the best way of storing them. Leather trousers (and skirts) are an exception. They have a tendency to "seat" and are often best stored rolled up to help them regain their shape. Belts are best stored hanging from the buckles – they are less likely to "crack" than if they are stored rolled up. The most efficient way of storing them is on a specially designed belt hanger.

**TIP**

I always use the polythene bags newly cleaned clothes come in, to protect clothes that I don't often wear – like evening wear. If travelling, I keep the clothes in the bags to help them remain crease-free.

When you are designing or choosing storage space for your bedroom, bear in mind that shelves in a cupboard are a lot more useful than drawers. Sweaters can get squashed and the fibres damaged when they are stored in drawers. Shelves are useful too, because you can see at a glance exactly what you have, rather than having to root about. Drawers and shelves should be lined so that splinters of wood do not damage clothes. Lavender sachets will keep your clothes sweet-smelling and moth-free.

To help your shoes retain their shape, put in shoe trees while they are still warm. Handbags are often sold with cotton bags for storage – keep these for continued protection in your own wardrobe.

Life can be made much more efficient if you store your clothes according to the seasons. In the moderate climate of Britain, for instance, there are roughly two "dressing" seasons – winter and summer – so you should move summer clothes to the most accessible spaces in the wardrobe or drawers in summer; the same with the winter selection in winter. Store the clothes that are out of season at the back of your wardrobe or somewhere else. This moving of your clothes twice a year is usually a good opportunity for your wardrobe evaluation.

## CLEANING CLOTHES

Bad dry-cleaning can curtail the life of a garment while first-rate cleaning will prolong it. I get most of my clothes dry-cleaned because, like many women, I'm short of time. I also think the professionals do it better! I always attach notes to the clothes, describing any stains and exactly what they are. It's also worth pointing out shoulder pads, otherwise you risk the garment being returned with two scrunched-up, cottonwool-like balls! If you are uncertain whether the buttons on a garment will survive dry-cleaning then mention this too, and a good dry-cleaner will remove them if necessary – similarly with belts.

The extent to which you dry-clean your clothes rather than wash them depends on your personal preference and your budget. Many women prefer to wash clothes because they feel that they are cleaner and smell fresher. Certainly, the worst sort of cleaners do not change the chemical solution very often so there is always the possibility

**DRY-CLEANING**

I am often asked whether "Dry-clean only" really means dry-clean only? The answer is that it doesn't. It is a protection for the manufacturer and the shop, against the people who throw everything in the washing machine and hope for the best. Many a time a customer has come in to Wardrobe, with a garment that has shrunk and told me it was washed using a top-quality powder by hand. I then discover, having sent it away for analysis, that it has been exposed to extreme heat (perhaps the heat of a washing machine?) When confronted, they've admitted that maybe their cleaning lady had put it in with the family wash. Back to the question. Unfortunately, if a garment does say "Dry-clean only" and you wash it by hand or in a machine, you run the risk of damaging it. Unless you're an expert on fabrics, don't attempt it without advice from your dry-cleaner. (If your dry-cleaner is any good, he should be able to give you washing instructions for most garments). Remember, clothes often look their best back from the dry-cleaners, not necessarily because of the cleaning but because they've been professionally pressed. This particularly applies to linen and silk.

147

that your clothes have been cleaned in rather dirty liquid that will give them a dull finish. When washing clothes, however, they still get a "beating", so always make sure that your washing powder has dissolved well and that you rinse thoroughly. Follow the advice on the garment, on your powder packet and on the washing machine instructions. If handwashing delicate fabrics, use delicate detergents. Use specialist cleaners for leather and suede.

> Clean shoes before you put them away rather than trying to find the necessary five minutes in the morning – the polish can be feeding the leather overnight.

Some cleaning companies will pick up clothes and then deliver them back. They are slightly more expensive than a high-street dry-cleaner but not as much as you might expect for such high standards and the convenience factor – a boon for the busy working woman. Beware of cleaning services in hotels; they are not always of a high standard.

148

## CLEANING SHOES

Keep bags and shoes regularly polished and use the most suitable products to clean them. If you can, always clean shoes before you put them away rather than trying to find the necessary five minutes in the morning – the polish can be feeding the leather overnight. Suede shoes can lose colour very quickly at the toe-caps. If they are black or dark brown, buy some suede dye and regularly dye that part of the shoe. The dye will also cover the toe-cap, which easily scuffs and fades. With light-coloured suede, there can be difficulty in matching the tone of dye to that of the shoes. So be careful.

## PRESSING

One of my most useful acquisitions has been a "pressing machine"; it's basically a steam box with an iron on it and is available from good department stores. You can use it to press vertically or horizontally, and I use it for all my clothes and my husband's suits.

Always check the underside of the iron for marks that may transfer to your clothes and, if possible, press everything inside out as this lessens the likelihood of creating shiny marks. Pressing sleeves can be quite tricky. Roll up a medium-sized towel and stuff it into the sleeve; you can then press the sleeve evenly all over so that it is

**TIP**

If something gets stained, resist the temptation to douse the stain with water. It is often more difficult to get the stain out afterwards and you may lose the colour from the fabric. Some cottons can even fade if splashed with water. Some of the stain-removing chemicals on the market now are quite effective. If you are uncertain and the garment is a cherished one, then opt for the best-dry-cleaning that you can afford.

free of unsightly creases. I also press leather skirts, to help them keep their shape – but very, very carefully, and turned inside out and with a towel over the leather. Spray starches are useful for crisping up cotton collar and cuffs and linen clothes. If your clothes could do with pressing, but you are in a hurry or have no iron, hang them in your bathroom at home or in your hotel room. The steam will help the creases to drop out. (Steam is also good for smoothing out velvet.) Never wear your clothes immediately after pressing them. If the fabric is still warm, it will crease very quickly indeed, undoing all your good work.

> Never wear your clothes immediately after pressing them. If the fabric is still warm, it will crease very quickly indeed, undoing all your good work.

Bows and trimmings on lingerie often wrinkle during washing. After you've squeezed the moisture out of your favourite bra and knickers, smooth out the bows and trimmings with your fingers so that they are lying flat. They should dry as new and need no further pressing.

If you really hate ironing or pressing, you can always find an enterprising person who is willing to do it for you – a service quite commonly available now.

## REPAIRS

Try to get repairs done as soon as they need doing. If you put them to one side, the next time you want to wear the garment you'll waste precious minutes making it presentable. Even small details, like a label coming undone, should be attended to, otherwise it could stick up above your collar. If a button drops off, sew it on as soon as possible or you'll lose it. Remember the saying, a stitch in time saves nine!

It's a good idea to keep a mini repair kit in the office, with some needles, thread in neutral colours (depending on the predominant shades in your wardrobe), safety pins and buttons. For safety, carry a duplicate in your toilet bag when travelling. For more serious repairs, there are places that do wonderful invisible mending so you don't have to throw out your favourite garment because it's damaged, or has been nibbled by a moth. Magazines and shops are good places for finding addresses for these menders.

**149**

### JEWELLERY CARE

Some people find that the best way to clean jewellery is by soaking it in some alcohol. Personally I find the battery-operated jewellery cleaners (together with jewellery cleaning solution) which are available from most department stores, are the most effective and safe method. For minor scratches, use an impregnated jewellery cloth (an ordinary polishing cloth won't do). Specify when buying a product whether you want it for gold or silver jewellery as there is a different cloth for each. These products promise to keep your jewellery sparkling!

# Useful Tips

*Confidence and being in control are the key to looking good. The tips below are designed to take the stress out of your life and put the style back in your wardrobe.*

## CLOTHES CARE

- Wear a scarf under your jacket collar especially in the morning to protect the fabric from make-up stains.
- Use lavender sachets and cedar wood in your wardrobe as effective moth repellents.
- To protect buttons during cleaning, ask your dry cleaner to cover each one with foil.
- Always reinforce the last button on a button-through dress. It will prevent the fabric from tearing.
- Don't hang up leather trousers and skirts. Roll them up instead. This helps maintain their shape.
- Always dry clean good clothes the first time they get dirty even if you can hand or machine-wash them. It preserves and "sets" the colour so it they won't fade when you wash the item afterwards.
- If something gets stained, resist the temptation to douse the stain with water, especially if the garment is only meant to be dry-cleaned. It will be difficult to get the stain out afterwards and you may lose the colour from the fabric.
- To clean fruit stains from washable fabrics, pour boiling water from at least 45cm (18in) onto the stain and then wash in the usual way.
- Remove chewing-gum from clothes by rubbing it with an ice cube and gently picking it off.
- Remove wax from clothes by placing brown paper over the wax and gently ironing over it. The wax will melt off the garment and into the paper.
- Never be tempted to remove pollen with a cloth. It will spread and stain. Instead, wrap sticky tape around the width of your hand, firmly press the tape onto the pollen and remove quickly.
- Don't polish shoes in the morning as fresh polish might rub off on your trousers. If you apply polish to shoes at night, it will slowly soak into the leather and feed it.

• Revive suede shoes by holding them over a steaming kettle, about 6 inches away from the steam.
• Make sure your fingernails are filed and your hands are smooth before putting on tights in order to avoid laddering them.

## TRAVELLING

• It is much easier to pack and coordinate your clothes when travelling if you only take black and brown shoes with you.
• Pack your clothes in dry-cleaning bags for crumple-free clothing.
• Always ask for Fragile labels when travelling – your luggage will be treated with greater care.
• If clothes become creased and you do not have access to an iron, turn on a hot shower or bath until the bathroom becomes full of steam then hang up your clothes. The creases will fall out overnight.
• If you paint your nails, don't forget to take varnish and remover with you to deal with flaking colour.

151

## YOUR PERSONAL APPEARANCE

• Never put clothes on immediately after ironing. They're still warm and will, therefore, crease easily.
• Always wear seam-free nude underwear under white clothing, not white underwear.
• If you rub hand cream gently over your tights once you have put them on, it will prevent fabrics from clinging to them.
• Buy the handbag that is in proportion to your size.
• Avoid flashy designer logo belt buckles. They date quickly and can look ostentatious.
• If you wear skirts, do not fall for the common assumption that wide hips and a large bottom can be disguised by wearing long, full or A-line skirts. A well-cut, straight and slightly tapered skirt worn to the knee is much more flattering.
• Tights with a Lycra content can improve the shape of the legs dramatically.
• Always keep a spare pair of tights in your handbag, desk drawer or car glove compartment. It's disconcerting to have to go to a meeting with a ladder in your tights.
• Make sure your bra fits properly. Sizes vary from manufacturer

to manufacturer so always try a bra on before you buy it.

- If your trousers seem to emphasize your thighs, ask a tailor to remove excess fabric from the front trouser pockets.

- Remember, if you're going to wear a dress or skirt after a day in trousers, roll down your socks or knee-highs in time for the markings from the socks to disappear from your legs. The same principle applies to bras and the marks they leave on your shoulders and across your back.

## CONFIDENCE BOOSTERS

- Whatever makes you feel wonderful, whatever boosts your mood, do it – whether it means wearing heels, buying a new lipstick, having a massage or wearing a different colour.

- Always dress for a job that is one position higher than the one you currently hold.

- Find your own "I'm fabulous garment". Determine what it is that you like about it and look for similar qualities in any new clothes that you plan to buy.

- Don't wear a new outfit for the first time to an important interview or meeting without having tried it on with all the right accessories and worn it for at least 15 minutes to check that it is comfortable and make sure you feel confident.

- Instead of saying "I'll buy the outfit when I get the job", think positively and buy the outfit to get the job.

- No matter how much you think you know about fashion, always be open to new ideas.

- Accentuate the positive, eliminate the negative.

- Don't wait until you've reached your goal weight to buy yourself a new outfit. Looking good on the very first day you decide to diet will immediately raise your self esteem and encourage you to reach your target weight.

## BUYING CLOTHES

- Beware of buying clothing with exaggerated shoulders – either very wide or very narrow – because they date quickly.

- Ignore the size that the label says the garment is. What matters is that you wear clothes that fit.

• Buy shoes one size bigger and use a half inner-sole to prevent your feet from being constricted should they swell up regularly, or if they have seriously pointed toes.

• If you buy a jacket made from a lightweight fabric, such as linen, allow for creasing, which will shorten the sleeves. This shortening effect applies to linen trousers and skirts too.

• When buying a jacket, always make sure that the last button does up over your hips.

• Extremes don't last in the world of fashion. Therefore, if you want an item to last, avoid bright colours and bold prints.

• Always try to shop in the morning when sales assistants are at their most awake and helpful.

• Before you sales shop, make a list of the things you really need and stick to it to avoid any impulse buys you may regret later.

• Before shopping for a garment to match a jacket, take a picture of yourself wearing the jacket to ensure that the proportions of the style of skirt or trousers you find are suitable.

• When trying on a garment, make sure you can see the back of yourself as well as the front. Ideally you should view yourself in a three-way mirror.

• Never shop when you're in a hurry, or feeling harassed  and never, never shop when you are depressed.

## HEALTH AND BEAUTY
• Try to buy a briefcase with handles as well as a shoulder strap to protect your back when the case is full and heavy.

• Alternate the heel height of your shoes as often as possible.

• Wear a shoe with a 3-4cm heel to add length to the leg and improve calf muscle. It should still be comfortable.

• Always use sunscreen if you are going outside, especially on your face. If you do this from an early age, you will be delighted how well your skin ages in comparison to skin which has gone unprotected.

• Rub a small amount of baby oil into the knee area to soften the skin and avoid crepey-ness as you age.

• Use neck cream at the back of the neck as well as the front.

• Always clean off all your makeup every night.

- Never pull or drag your skin when removing make-up as this will encourage wrinkles. Use soft, upward strokes.
- Avoid smoking as it wreaks havoc on your skin.
- Exercise will get rid of puffiness in your face and open up your pores.
- Moisturize every morning and evening to ensure an elastic, healthy skin. Apply a richer cream at night when the skin does most of its "repair" work.
- Give creams and lotions a few minutes to be absorbed before you apply your make-up.
- Use non-oily make-up remover. It does not aggravate the skin and the make-up can be removed with gentle strokes. It also allows you to reapply make-up soon afterwards if needed.
- Use the right cleanser for your skin. For oily skin use a gentle cleanser. For normal-to-dry skin use a creamy cleanser that washes off easily.
- On holiday, use a gel cleanser rather than a creamy one, to combat heat and humidity.
- If you have oily skin, avoid toners containing alcohol as they block impurities below the surface. Over-drying the skin is a common mistake made by women with oily skin.
- Products containing AHAs (Alpha Hydroxy Acids, from milk, sugarcane and apples) exfoliate the skin without leaving the flakiness or redness associated with grainy scrubs. They can be used for all skin-types and are especially useful for treating blackheads, dehydrated skin and an uneven skin texture. Start with a gentle formula to make sure you do not have an adverse reaction.
- If the skin around your eyes is dry, apply eye cream before you apply concealer.
- If you have fine lines under your eyes, avoid using concealer as it emphasizes wrinkles. If you must, use a light-textured, light-reflective product, which minimizes lines. Do the same for your foundation. Avoid anything that is too matte as this will also emphasize lines.
- Powder over foundation or concealer is the secret to keeping long-lasting, smudge-free make-up.
- Loose powder is more effective than pressed powder although it

gets messy. Pressed powder is more convenient if you are out, but it lies more heavily and can deaden a delicate, dry complexion.

• Use oil-free make-up if your skin is oily and prone to breaking out. If it is dry, look for make-up with moisturiser. Powdery make-up, including eye pencil, is more suitable for older skin.

• You can apply eyeshadow as eyeliner if you moisten your brush to apply it.

• Lip pencil creates a wax barrier and prevents your lipstick from seeping.

• Keep your hands away from your face – you will be transferring dirt to your skin and inadvertently wiping off your make-up. When using the phone, keep it away from your face for the same reason.

## USEFUL TIPS

• Five minutes spent every night deciding what to wear the next day and sorting out what you need, is five minutes well spent.

• Carry a spare pair of tights with you so that you are never wearing tights with holes or ladders.

• If you haven't worn a garment for three years give it to someone who will wear it.

• Always remember, LESS IS MORE. Do you really need another pair of black trousers?

## CLOTHING SIZES

All size equivalents are approximate. Depending on cut, you may find that you are a size above or below what you expect to be. Glove sizes are the same in every country.

SUITS AND DRESSES

| | | | | | | |
|---|---|---|---|---|---|---|
| American | 8 | 10 | 12 | 14 | 16 | 18 |
| British | 10 | 12 | 14 | 16 | 18 | 20 |
| European | 38 | 40 | 42 | 44 | 46 | 48 |

SHOES

| | | | | | | |
|---|---|---|---|---|---|---|
| American | $6\frac{1}{2}$ | 7 | $7\frac{1}{2}$ | 8 | $8\frac{1}{2}$ | 9 |
| British | $4\frac{1}{2}$ | 5 | $5\frac{1}{2}$ | 6 | $6\frac{1}{2}$ | 7 |
| European | $37\frac{1}{2}$ | 38 | 39 | $39\frac{1}{2}$ | 40 | $40\frac{1}{2}$ |

# WARDROBE

*For further information about the
shop seminars and consultancy contact:*

Wardrobe

42 Conduit Street
London W1R 9FB

Telephone 0207 494 1131

# Index

158

159

My sincere thanks to everyone involved in this book – I am delighted with the result.

There are a few special 'thank yous' I would like to say:

To Mum and Dad for their love and understanding – I know that as a child I drove them mad with my very determined views on appearance.

My sons, Richard and James, and my grandson Charlie – may he never have to wash plastic hangers like his father and uncle!

Catherine Baudrand, who collaborated with me in the writing and development of this book, and with whom I enjoyed working so much.

My friend Joy, the rest of the Wardrobe team, and my PA Michéle for constantly being there.

Clare Currie from Marshall Editions for her true involvement, inspiration and continual care.

Lingerie by Sculpture, 23 Brook Street, London W1

Glasses by Vision Care, 70 Baker Street, London W1

Additional glasses by Modis and Sàfilo UK

Make-up by Maggie Hunt. Cosmetics supplied by Bobbi Brown, Bourgeois, Cosmetics à la Carte, Estée Lauder, Lancôme and Shisheido

Hair at the Wardrobe Hair Studio, beauty by Frances Hall, energy and relaxation by Maxwell Forsyth, nutrition by Eleanor Burton all at Sfera House, 42 Conduit Street, London W1

Mannequins supplied by Proportion

Illustrations: by Penny Sobr, cover, pp 3, 12-13, 44-45, 70-71, 102-3, 128-9, 160

Photography: All by Iain Bagwell, except pp27b, 31c, 32, 46-47, 48-49, 52-53, 56-57, 67c, 68, 74, 95c, 96, 111c, 112, 122, 125c, 126 by Andrew Sydenham; pp 51, 55, 62-63, 64-65, 139, 133 by Martin Evening.

Index: Judi Barstow

Additional styling by the Wardrobe Team

**160**

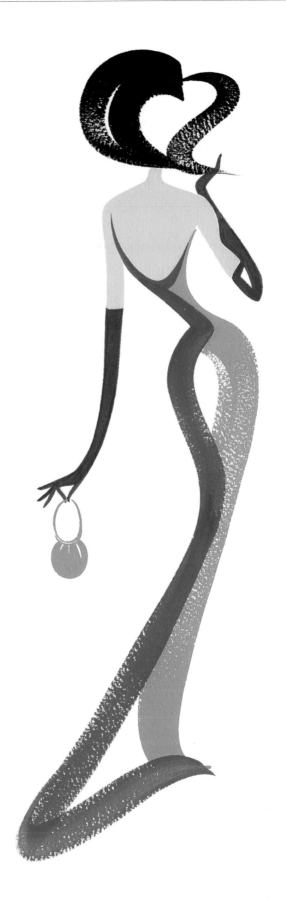